Education and Society

ISSUES

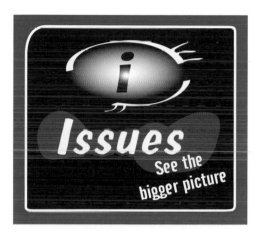

Volume 209

Series Editor

Lisa Firth

Independence

Educational Publishers

First published by Independence

The Studio, High Green

Great Shelford

Cambridge CB22 5EG

England

© Independence 2011

British Library Cataloguing in Publication Data

Education and society. -- (Issues ; v. 209)

1. Education and state--Great Britain. 2. Education--

Great Britain.

I. Series II. Firth, Lisa.

379.4'1-dc22

ISBN-13: 978 1 86168 585 8

Printed in Great Britain

MWL Print Group Ltd

CONTENTS

Chapter 1 School Issues

Chapter 2 Higher Education

OTHER TITLES IN THE ISSUES SERIES

For more on these titles, visit: www.independence.co.uk

A note on critical evaluation

Because the information reprinted here is from a number of different sources, readers should bear in mind the origin of the text and whether the source is likely to have a particular bias when presenting information (just as they would if undertaking their own research). It is hoped that, as you read about the many aspects of the issues explored in this book, you will critically evaluate the information presented. It is important that you decide whether you are being presented with facts or opinions. Does the writer give a biased or an unbiased report? If an opinion is being expressed, do you agree with the writer?

Education and Society offers a useful starting point for those who need convenient access to information about the many issues involved. However, it is only a starting point. Following each article is a URL to the relevant organisation's website, which you may wish to visit for further information.

Attitudes to learning

Edge Annual Programme of Stakeholder Surveys: report summary.

A report by YouGov Plc, commissioned by the Edge Foundation

This annual survey measures the extent and type of education-employer partnerships around the UK, looking at the perceptions of the value of employer engagement, levels of awareness about the opportunities and types of activities available, any barriers to partnership and perceptions about vocational qualifications. Researchers carried out fieldwork from Sept-Oct 2009, receiving responses from 2,198 young people, 1,013 parents, 1,001 employers and 1,034 teachers (covering Key Stages 3 to 5). Data was weighted for a high number of variables, including gender, age, school/college type, current activity (e.g. working full time, on a training course), industry and government office region.

Different types of learning in schools

Stakeholders* continue to believe that schools favour academic qualifications over vocational ones. Half of secondary teachers and 39 per cent of parents said their school favoured academic qualifications, with very few saying it favoured vocational ones. However, large proportions (around four in ten) also thought it balanced between the two. By contrast with school, sixth form/FE colleges are seen as much more balanced, with the majority (57 per cent) of lecturers saying their college had a balanced view. These opinions have not changed significantly since the 2008 research.

The results show a continuing concern over the balance between specialising and a generalist approach. Teachers believe that the education system forces children to continue with subjects which do not benefit them (net agreement scores of 43 per cent). This is not significantly different from last year; however, independent school teachers in particular have become less likely to agree with this view. Many parents believe that the system forces children to narrow their options too early (net agreement score of 41).

Teachers continue to feel confident that they understand their students, showing no change since last year. Children at Key Stage 3 continue in general to feel

understood by their teachers, and compared with last year are slightly less likely to disagree that their teacher knows what they like and don't like at school, showing a small-scale improvement.

As in 2008, the majority (60 per cent) of children are involved in practical learning often at Key Stage 3; however, this drops to around half by Key Stage 4. While many children thought that the level was about right, there continues to be demand for more practical learning at both key stages. However, young people at Key Stage 4 were slightly less likely to say there are too few practical projects this year than last (46 per cent compared with 55 per cent), despite reporting the same amount of practical learning. This higher level of satisfaction is driven primarily by girls rather than boys. Parents also continue to feel there is too little practical learning, but were slightly less likely to say this than in 2008. Teachers were the group most satisfied with the level of practical learning, but 39 per cent still thought that there was too little.

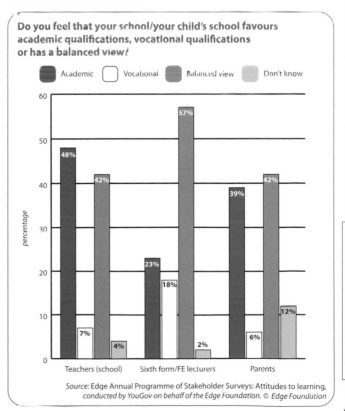

Source: Edge Annual Programme of Stakeholder Surveys: Attitudes to learning, conducted by YouGov on behalf of the Edge Foundation. © Edge Foundation

EDGE FOUNDATION

Teachers and parents expressed a strong opinion that a reduction in practical learning would have negative impacts, in particular on readiness for further/higher education, learning speed and levels of interest in school. Two thirds (65 per cent) of teachers thought students would generally be less ready for the workplace if practical learning were reduced, while 57 per cent thought students would be less interested in school. However, 23 per cent of teachers also thought young people would be better prepared for university, showing a concern among some teachers that practical learning may take time away from 'the basics' of education.

Parents (with a child who prefers practical learning or a mixture of academic and practical) voiced similar concerns to teachers. Around half thought their child would be less happy if practical learning were reduced, and around a third that they would learn more slowly. However, as with teachers, there was also a concern over readiness for the next stage; 15 per cent said their child would be better prepared for further or higher education.

The results suggest that teachers may feel better equipped to support practical learning than last year. However, since the question format was not identical, this should be considered as indicative only.

Schools' top priorities continue to be helping children to achieve their potential (85 per cent), performance in qualifications (80 per cent) and increasing confidence (77 per cent). So far, the economic climate has not significantly impacted on priorities regarding workplace readiness or university.

Attitudes to different types of learning

A mixture of academic and practical learning continues to be the most popular option at both key stages, although, as with last year, the results show that the popularity of academic learning increases between Key Stages 3 and 4. However, at Key Stage 3, parents were significantly more likely this year to say their child prefers to learn academically (22 per cent compared with 15 per cent in 2008), although they were not significantly less likely to choose any other individual option. At Key Stage 4, there was also an indicative (but not statistically significant) increase in those saying their child prefers to learn academically. Children at both key stages continue to support a mixture of learning types; however, there is more support overall for options relating to practical learning than ones relating to academic learning.

There were few very significant changes to attitudes around vocational qualifications. All groups continued to believe on balance that vocational learning provides a good education and often leads to a good career, with employers generally the most positive. However, teachers have become slightly less positive on

vocational learning providing a good education, while children and young people have become slightly more positive on this.

Stakeholders do not generally believe that vocational learning is only for those who don't do well at school, with only between a sixth and a quarter agreeing with this. Children and young people were slightly more likely to agree but also slightly more likely to disagree, therefore their overall opinion has not changed; however, the results suggest they may be slightly better informed about vocational qualifications compared with last year. Employers have become slightly more positive on this measure, while the view of parents and teachers have remained constant.

As in 2008, most stakeholders do not believe that young people will only fulfil their potential by going to university. Teachers, employers and children and young people have all become slightly less likely on balance to hold this view than last year (although the differences are small). However, parents, the group most likely to believe this, have not changed their opinion since last year; a quarter still believe that university is the only suitable route for young people.

Despite generally positive views of vocational qualifications, many stakeholders continue to believe that taking such qualifications may rule out university as an option. Around a third of young people and employers, and slightly more parents and teachers, agreed with this view. Teachers have become slightly more likely to believe this than in 2008, while young people have become indicatively less likely. Around a quarter to a third of each group expressed no opinion, suggesting that understanding of the progression route from vocational qualifications may remain limited for some stakeholders.

There is a continuing belief among many children and young people that academic qualifications are more important than vocational ones; however, views in this area have changed since the 2008 survey. At Key Stage 4, young people have become less likely to see academic qualifications as more important (36 per cent compared with 44 per cent) and more likely to see the two types as equally important (50 per cent compared with 43 per cent). Key Stage 4 children were also more likely to think their parents valued both types equally and less likely to think they favoured academic qualifications, although this may reflect the change in their own views rather than actual change on the part of parents. At Key Stage 3, by contrast, there was an indicative shift towards favouring academic qualifications, although this development is not statistically significant so far.

Employers continued to have a balanced view of different qualification types, with little change since last year's research. Similar proportions chose academic and vocational as most important, and the largest group (44 per cent) thought both equally important. The results continue to show a large variation by business size, with smaller organisations more in favour of vocational qualifications, and larger ones more in favour of academic. Medium-sized organisations were indicatively more likely to favour vocational qualifications compared with last year.

Employers believe many soft skills are better developed by vocational qualifications; these include team working, business and customer awareness, and attitude and enthusiasm. However, academic qualifications are believed to be better for developing numeracy, communication and literacy, and basic IT skills. These results show little change since last year, although the proportion thinking vocational qualifications are better at developing business and customer awareness has decreased slightly (from 54 to 49 per cent). There is a continuing perception among some teachers that vocational qualifications are mainly suited to less able individuals. More than a third (37 per cent) believed this of NVQs/SVQs, and 31 per cent of qualifications such as BTECs and City and Guilds. This shows no change since 2008. Although take-up of apprenticeships has increased, teachers' view of them has not improved. Awareness of Diplomas has increased only slightly, and views among those who are aware have not changed significantly.

January 2010

⇨ The above information is an extract from the report *Edge Annual Programme of Stakeholder Surveys: Attitudes to Learning*, conducted by YouGov on behalf of the Edge Foundation, and is reprinted with permission. Visit www.edge.co.uk for more information.

© Edge Foundation

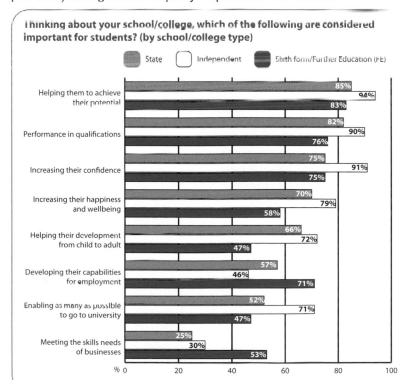

Thinking about your school/college, which of the following are considered important for students? (by school/college type)

State | Independent | Sixth form/Further Education (FE)

Helping them to achieve their potential: 85%, 94%, 83%
Performance in qualifications: 82%, 90%, 76%
Increasing their confidence: 75%, 91%, 75%
Increasing their happiness and wellbeing: 70%, 79%, 58%
Helping their development from child to adult: 66%, 72%, 47%
Developing their capabilities for employment: 57%, 46%, 71%
Enabling as many as possible to go to university: 52%, 71%, 47%
Meeting the skills needs of businesses: 25%, 30%, 53%

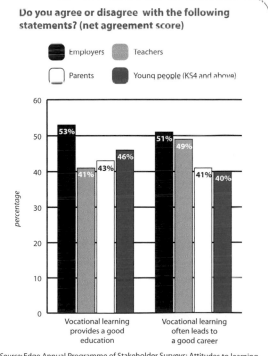

Do you agree or disagree with the following statements? (net agreement score)

Employers | Teachers | Parents | Young people (KS4 and above)

Vocational learning provides a good education: 53%, 41%, 43%, 46%
Vocational learning often leads to a good career: 51%, 49%, 41%, 40%

Source: Edge Annual Programme of Stakeholder Surveys: Attitudes to learning, conducted by YouGov on behalf of the Edge Foundation. © Edge Foundation 2010

EDGE FOUNDATION

Pushy parents turn schools into 'exam factories'

Private schools are being turned into 'exam factories' amid pressure from pushy parents to produce decent results, according to research.

By Graeme Paton

Teachers are being put under considerable pressure by families to deliver top exam grades to boost children's chances of getting into the best universities.

Research commissioned by the Headmasters' and Headmistresses' Conference, which represents 250 leading independent schools, said the focus on GCSE and A-level preparation compromised their ability to deliver sport, expeditions and school trips for final-year pupils.

The study – published at HMC's annual meeting in central London – said pressure from parents and universities produced a vicious circle that constrained schools' abilities to provide a broad education and teach children to think independently.

It said many schools were risk averse and lacked the courage to actively create the curriculum that most teachers wanted to deliver.

The disclosure follows claims from Gary Lineker, the BBC presenter and former England football captain, that Charterhouse treated his son as a guinea pig by ditching A-levels in favour of new-style exams.

George Lineker, 18, failed to obtain the three B grades needed to get into Manchester University after the fee-paying school in Surrey switched to the tougher Cambridge Pre-U qualification.

In the latest report, academics from London University's Institute of Education, interviewed staff and students from 68 schools about the curriculum for 13- to 19-year-olds.

It said: 'Despite the desire to pursue broad educational aims and purposes, participants felt under considerable pressure from parents and students to deliver the best possible examination results in a highly competitive market.'

They perceived that this was exacerbated by the actions of the 'top universities', who not only demand high grades at A-levels but also use GCSE A* grades as selection tools for certain courses, such as medicine, dentistry and law.

The effects of these combined pressures was to create not only tensions, for example, between preparing young people to get into the top universities and preparing them for life and employment, but also a climate of instrumentalism and cynicism in which they felt they were being turned into exam factories.

Many private schools have been hugely critical of reforms to GCSEs and A-levels, which have been broken down into bite-sized modules that students can re-sit to boost their overall grade.

Some schools are moving towards alternative linear courses – such as the Pre-U – in which students take final exams after two years of study.

Many private schools have been hugely critical of reforms to GCSEs and A-levels

But the latest report warned that anti-modular sentiment was more widespread than anti-modular action because of the continued support for more regular assessment among students.

Professor Ken Spours, one of the report's co-authors, said the top eight universities had a distorting effect on the curriculum and the exams system by demanding a string of A* and A grades at GCSE and A-level as a condition of entry.

It comes amid record competition for university places. Some 210,000 candidates are believed to have been rejected from degree courses in 2010 following a surge in applications during the economic downturn.

The report – *The 13-19 Education in HMC Schools* – said: Despite all the rhetoric, many [schools] were risk averse and lacked the courage to actively create the curriculum space that the majority maintained they wanted to develop.

Researchers insisted that fee-paying schools did offer a wide range of extra-curricular activities, but added: 'Even here the increasing focus on health and safety issues and the effects of the examination system in the final year of both GCSE and A-level means that sport, expeditions and trips have been compromised.'

28 September 2010

THE TELEGRAPH

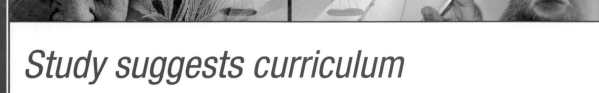

Study suggests curriculum 'overloaded' and 'narrow'

The national curriculum in England is in need of reform, according to a new report.

By Dorothy Lepkowska

A study from Cambridge University found that teachers had been forced into a 'tick-list' approach to teaching, which had resulted in pupils being coached to pass exams and tests.

However, Cambridge Assessment warned against making wholesale changes based on international models as this would have to take into account local contexts and could lead to 'unnecessary disruption' to the education system.

Michael Gove, the Education Secretary, who wrote the foreword to the research, has suggested that international evidence should be at the heart of curriculum reform.

The study was written by Tim Oates, group director of assessment, research and development at Cambridge Assessment, who concluded there were 'significant structural problems' in the national curriculum 'which need to be corrected'.

A study from Cambridge University found that teachers had been forced into a 'tick-list' approach to teaching

He said that changing the content of what is taught would not in itself improve standards and other factors needed to be considered, including the quality of teaching, levels of teacher expertise, availability and quality of teaching materials, and inspection.

Mr Oates, an advisor to the Government on curriculum reform, argued that a well-defined and enhanced national curriculum based on concepts, principles and key knowledge could lead to a greater focus on deeper learning, with fewer topics being pursued to greater depth.

However, his report, *Could do better: Using International Comparisons to Refine the National Curriculum in England*, found that the national curriculum had been effective in raising standards, improving pupil progression and had led to higher expectations for young people.

He suggested it would be important to use international comparisons when reviewing the national curriculum, but he advised against importing any system in its entirety because the contexts in which they were working varied. International perspectives helped to achieve 'a principled reduction of any unnecessary bulk in the national curriculum', though he warned 'it cannot do everything. To expect it so to do will most likely result in failure.'

Mr Gove has often cited Finland's national curriculum as a model of what children should be expected to learn and achieve. In his foreword to the study he said the paper offered 'a concise analysis of some of the problems with our current national curriculum and helps explain why so many other nations are outpacing us in educational performance.

'The best-performing education nations deliberately set out to compare themselves against international benchmarks – learning from each other and constantly asking what is required to help all children do better.

'Shortly, my department will launch its own review of the national curriculum and the remit will explicitly, for the first time, require benchmarking against the most successful school systems.

'This has to be done with great care to avoid learning the wrong lessons from countries with very different cultures. But it is essential if we are to keep pace with the world's best.'

25 November 2010

SECED

Adapt GCSE to be national exam at 14

Information from the Sutton Trust.

A proposal that the GCSE should be adapted to become a national examination for 14-year-olds is made by Professor Alan Smithers and Dr Pamela Robinson of the University of Buckingham in a report published today by the Sutton Trust, which commissioned their research comparing education systems in the 30 countries of the OECD.

Professor Smithers and Dr Robinson at the Centre for Education and Employment Research conclude that there are lessons for the new Coalition Government from international comparisons of admissions to, and the structure of, the 'lower' and 'upper' stages of secondary education.

England remains an outlier on the international stage in terms of the different educational pathways offered to children during their formative years

26 of the 30 OECD countries have a clear array of pathways in the later years of schooling, spanning pre-university, technical training and preparation for employment. In the USA, Canada and New Zealand the pathways open up post school. England with its untidy mix is a conspicuous exception. The authors say that the Government could make 'education 14-19' a reality by moving and adapting the GCSE to become the national examination for 14-year-olds. 'This would then become the natural starting point for an array of awards taking young people in different directions. If these were sufficiently attractive, young people would want to stay on for as long as it took to gain a qualification and there would be no need for the sticks necessary to impose compulsory staying on.

While such a major reform may be a step too far for the Government, the Sutton Trust believes that clearer educational options from age 14 onwards are needed to ensure that children from non-privileged backgrounds pursue the choices that genuinely reflect their interests and abilities.

On admissions, the authors challenge the Government to decide how they want pupils to be distributed across secondary education. Proximity to the school promotes social divisions. Countering this by balloting or random allocation would be unpopular electorally. Selection at 11 on educational merit carries a lot of emotional baggage.

They conclude that 'It would not be necessary for the Government to determine centrally if it allowed schools to set their own enrolment policies.' It could follow the example of New Zealand (where there is unregulated choice though pupils are assured of a place in a local school), or it could go the whole hog and allow state schools the same freedoms as independent schools.

The Sutton Trust continues to believe that a national admissions framework that applies to all schools is necessary.

Responding to the report, Sir Peter Lampl, chairman of the Sutton Trust, said:

'England remains an outlier on the international stage in terms of the different educational pathways offered to children during their formative years – and effectively we have differentiation by default: all too often children's choices are dictated by the school they happen to be in, not their own talents and interests.

'Professor Smithers and Dr Robinson propose a radical solution to bring England into line with international practice: undertake national examinations at age 14 instead of age 16, and offer pupils a set of distinct and credible educational routes thereafter.'

22 November 2010

⇨ The above information is reprinted with kind permission from the Sutton Trust. Visit www.suttontrust.com for more information.

SUTTON TRUST

Are our schools really failing?

Information from The Truth About Our Schools.

By Fiona Miller

The received wisdom in parts of the media is as follows:

➔ State schools are getting worse.

➔ The £37 billion spent on them (a 74% increase in real terms) since 1997 has been wasted.

➔ There was once a 'golden age' when grammar schools reigned supreme, giving poor children ladders out of poverty and into the best universities, and all our people were educated to a higher standard than they are today.

In 1959, at the height of the 'golden age':

➔ 9% of 16-year-olds got five O-levels.

➔ More than a third of grammar school pupils only got three O-levels.

➔ Fewer than 10% of the population went to university and most came from professional or managerial homes.

➔ Most children were failed by the 11-plus test and sent to secondary modern schools which often didn't have sixth forms.

Fast forward to today:

➔ In 2010, 69% of 16-year-olds got five good GCSEs, up from 45% in 1997.

➔ In the most recent report from Ofsted 68% of schools were judged good or outstanding. 8% were unsatisfactory.

➔ In 2010, around 80% of children left primary school at the required level in maths and English, up from just over 60% in 1997.

➔ Almost 40% of young people now go to university and, even though the gap in attainment and university access between children from the best and worse off homes is still too great, teenagers from the poorest homes are 50% more likely to go to university than they were 15 years ago.

State school access to Oxford and Cambridge is also frequently used as an example of falling standards in state schools. But contrary to popular, and media, myth, the number of state school pupils getting into Oxford and Cambridge has risen steadily since the 1960s, coinciding with a greater percentage of the population attending comprehensive schools. The evidence is presented clearly in a research note on Oxbridge elitism from the House of Commons library.

➔ A survey for the Robbins Report in 1961 found that 34% of all students from Oxford and 27% at Cambridge came from state schools.

➔ Rates of entry to both institutions from state schools had increased to more than 50% by the late 1990s.

➔ In 2009, 58% of pupils at Cambridge and 53.9% of pupils at Oxford came from state schools.

➔ The acceptance rate for state schools pupils in 2009 was 24% at Cambridge and 22.4% at Oxford although varied by college.

➔ The acceptance rate for independent school pupils was 29.8% at Oxford in 2009 and 30% at Cambridge in 2009.

In the most recent report from Ofsted 68% of schools were judged good or outstanding, 8% were unsatisfactory

---

Overall, the evidence seems clear. State schools are improving and giving greater opportunities to more young people in contrast to the supposed 'golden age' when only an elite minority prospered at school. Clearly there are people who preferred it that way and may well resent the opportunities presented to children other than their own.

A common response to the evidence of improvement is that exams have become dumbed down in the last 30 years and qualifications easier to gain, therefore the improvement is only illusory. For a good dispassionate look at what exams were really like in the golden age of elite education, read *State Schools since the 1950s: the Good News* by former head teacher and Ofsted inspector Adrian Elliott or follow his excellent series debunking educational myths in the *TES* which looked at exam papers over the last decade and revealed how dull and unchallenging many old O- and A-level questions were.

For another, more in-depth look at exam standards see the Curriculum and Qualifications Development Agency website, which commissioned independent research on this subject and concluded that by and large the exam system was in good shape.

THE TRUTH ABOUT OUR SCHOOLS

It is always worth remembering that it isn't only the questions that determine exams results but also the way they are marked, so all those armchair pundits who can remember exactly what was in their O-level English paper 40 years ago are only telling half the story.

In 2010, 69% of 16-year-olds got five good GCSEs, up from 45% in 1997

Today's secondary school pupils work much harder than my generation did in the early 70s. Teachers are also much more focused on educating students in how to pass exams, partly as a result of the pressure of league tables. That may raise questions about the nature of schooling today and whether it is just an exam treadmill leaving no room for enjoyment or creativity, but it shouldn't detract from the significant successes of young people, and their teachers, when judged by the criteria successive governments have set for them.

⇨ The above information is reprinted with kind permission from The Truth About Our Schools. Visit their website at www.thetruthaboutourschools.com for more information.

© Fiona Miller

Education: key facts and figures worldwide

Information from Oxfam.

⇨ 72 million children are currently out of school, the majority of whom are girls.

⇨ There are at least 771 million illiterate adults worldwide, of whom 64 per cent are women.

⇨ Two of the UN Millennium Development Goals (MDGs) relate directly to education. MDG 2 aims to achieve universal primary education by 2015, ensuring that children everywhere, boys and girls alike, will be able to complete a full course of primary schooling. MDG 3 – to promote gender equality and empower women – seeks to eliminate gender disparity in education. Its first target was to get as many girls as boys into school by 2005.

⇨ The first MDG target – to get as many girls as boys into primary and secondary school by 2005 – was missed in over 90 countries. In countries such as Niger and Burkina Faso, only one in three girls go to school at all.

⇨ In 2006, failure to reach the 2005 MDG gender-parity target will result in over one million unnecessary child and maternal deaths. Educated women have greater knowledge about health issues and greater bargaining power in the household, which has a positive impact on their own health and that of their children.

⇨ HIV/AIDS infection rates double among young people who do not finish primary school. If every girl and boy received a complete primary education, at least seven million new cases of HIV could be prevented in a decade.

⇨ In many countries, school fees are a major barrier that prevents children – especially girls – from going to school. When school fees were abolished in Uganda, Tanzania and Kenya, seven million additional children – many of them girls – entered school in these three countries alone.

⇨ Well-trained and well-supported teachers are essential to providing good-quality education for girls and boys. However, there is currently a global shortage of two million teachers, and at least 15 million new teachers will be needed between now and 2015 in order to achieve education for all.

⇨ Globally, an extra $7-17 billion per year is still needed to enable all girls and boys to receive a quality primary education.

⇨ The above information from Education: key facts and figures [http://www.oxfam.org.uk/resources/issues/education/key_facts.html], 17 February 2011, is reproduced with the permission of Oxfam GB, Oxfam House, John Smith Drive, Cowley, Oxford OX4 2JY, UK www.oxfam.org.uk. Oxfam GB does not necessarily endorse any text or activities that accompany the materials.

© Oxfam

Myth: standards rise is just exams getting easier

Is the educational bar really being lowered?

By Adrian Elliott

Continuing our series confronting enduring school myths, Adrian Elliott, a former headteacher and inspector, examines whether the educational bar is really being lowered.

The most common charge against modern schools is that standards have not risen and any supposed improvement has been due simply to examinations getting easier. Proponents of this view have gone to some lengths to prove their point.

Unfortunate 16-year-olds were whisked off to a mock 1950s grammar school by Channel 4 and given old O-level papers so their subsequent failure could be paraded before the nation. The Conservatives intend to publish exam papers back to Victorian days on their website, while comparisons of old and new papers appear regularly in the national press.

Yet such exercises have a number of flaws, which seem obvious – remarkably so – given the stress placed by those responsible on academic rigour. I am not referring to the sheer dishonesty of giving pupils four weeks' preparation for exam papers for which the original candidates had two years, or the common practice of comparing the toughest questions from the past and the easiest ones from modern papers. No, much more significant – and fallacious – is the assumption that the standards of national cohorts of children can be judged entirely by exam questions.

Surely, two other factors are at least as significant: what proportion of these cohorts actually sat the exams? And how well did they cope? The answers, in the so-called golden age of the 1950s, were not very many and pretty badly.

Only the very brightest pupils sat O- or A-levels then – a fraction of the number who now sit public exams – and yet they failed in droves. Examiners were unimpressed by the efforts of this select group. Particularly striking is their concern about the large numbers who simply should never have been entered for the examinations, at both levels.

In 1957, an English literature O-level report concluded that 'too many candidates ... were unable to understand the question paper', while a 1960 A-level maths report also complained that 'many candidates clearly had no understanding of the subject matter of most questions'. A literature O-level report in 1956 noted that 'whole groups are entered in which no more than a quarter have any chance of passing'.

Crucially, the examiners stressed these were not isolated instances. They were discussing, remember, England's brightest youngsters. Yet if the top set in an average comprehensive school today were to be prepared for a 1950s O-level paper, would a quarter fail? And most modern top sets contain a wider range of ability than grammar schools in the past.

Furthermore, were papers in the past really as difficult as their selective use by national newspapers suggests?

> **The number of students achieving five or more GCSEs at grade C or above is now more than eight times the number getting five O-levels before the spread of comprehensive education**

Dr Peter Knight, a university vice-chancellor, comments that a 'great wodge of the material I did at A-level (maths) is no longer on the syllabus and rightly so: some of the material regarded as degree level in the 1960s is now on the A-level syllabus'.

English language O-level papers would appear laughable to its target group today, the brightest 20 per cent. Essay titles from the 1959 paper, which I sat, included 'Pleasures of life in a large town', 'Washing day' and 'Coach tours'. Candidates were asked to explain the meaning of 'humility' and show the alternative meanings of words such as 'vice' and 'lap'. Is this truly beyond today's brightest 16-year-olds?

Even if critics were correct and examinations had become easier, this would hardly 'prove' that overall standards had dropped. One would need to determine by how much the standard had fallen in relation to the numbers taking the exam. If a GCSE grade C is really easier to obtain today than a pass at O-level in 1960, is it twice, three or four times as easy? A fourfold difference seems unlikely, implying a modern student achieving 80 per cent at GCSE, prepared properly for the O-level examination, would only get 20 per cent.

Yet the number of students achieving five or more GCSEs at grade C or above is now more than eight times the number getting five O-levels before the spread of comprehensive education. This increase cannot possibly be explained away by any 'lowering' of the standard of the examination.

The percentage of girls achieving A-levels rose almost 400 per cent from the cohort born in the 1940s to that of the 1960s

Detailed, subject-by-subject research by the Schools Curriculum and Assessment Authority and its successor, the Qualifications and Curriculum Authority (QCA), has not shown evidence of the wholesale slippage in standards assumed so readily by critics. Cambridge Assessment has looked at standards over time in both Key Stage 2 and Key Stage 4 English. It found that 'the experimental evidence from all subjects and key stages indicated that there has been a substantial real improvement in children's achievement'. Although they thought national tests had exaggerated the extent of the improvement (due to teaching to the test), there had still been 'significant gains in achievement'.

Another comparison by Cambridge Assessment of GCSE English scripts of 2004 with those of 1993 and 1994, and with O-level scripts in 1980, indicated an overall improvement in standards. Spelling was better in 1980 than in either the 1990s or in 2004, but in all other respects – content, writing, vocabulary and punctuation – the scripts of 2004 were better than those of 1993 and 1994, and as good (if not better) than those of 1980, when far fewer pupils took the examination. Significantly, the improvements had taken place at all levels, not just among the brightest pupils.

Those who say there has been no real improvement in school standards also seem to happily ignore half the population. Can critics really deny that the educational levels achieved by girls have risen massively over the past 30 to 50 years? The reasons may lie partly beyond the school gates, but there is overwhelming evidence that girls have made enormous progress at every stage from pre-primary to higher education. Furthermore, international studies have demonstrated that one of the biggest determinants of a child's success at school is the educational level attained by its mother, especially in higher secondary education.

The percentage of girls achieving A-levels rose almost 400 per cent from the cohort born in the 1940s to that of the 1960s, most the products of comprehensive education. Many of the latter now have children who

have taken, or are approaching, GCSEs or A-levels. In the light of this, why is it so surprising that there has been an explosion both in the numbers taking public examinations and of those achieving higher grades? For all the allegations of deliberately lowered standards, the improvement was predictable and should surely be welcomed and built upon.

Adrian Elliott is the author of *State Schools Since the 1950s: the Good News* (Trentham Books)

And the results are in...

⇨ In 1959, around nine per cent of 16-year-olds got five or more O-levels. In 2009, the proportion gaining five or more GCSEs was 70 per cent.

⇨ Essay titles in the English O-level paper in 1959 included 'Pleasures of life in a large town', 'Washing day' and 'Coach tours'.

⇨ Essay titles in the 2009 OCR English GCSE included: 'How do you present different images of yourself in different situations and why do you do so?'

⇨ A recent survey showed that most 55- to 65-year-olds lack the maths skills expected of a nine-year-old today.

⇨ An examiners' report on O-level English literature in 1956 noted that 'whole groups are entered in which no more than a quarter have any chance of passing'.

International studies have demonstrated that one of the biggest determinants of a child's success at school is the educational level attained by its mother especially in higher secondary education

This year's OCR examiners' report on English GCSE stated that examiners were 'very impressed with the overall quality of the entry in this session and there was general agreement that standards were higher than on any other occasion'. It added: 'Many grizzled examiners found themselves astonished at the levels of emotional maturity and sophisticated understanding displayed by 15- and 16-year-old candidates in a 45-minute exam.'

⇨ The above information is reprinted with kind permission from the *Times Educational Supplement*. Visit www.tes.co.uk for more information.

© *Times Educational Supplement*

TIMES EDUCATIONAL SUPPLEMENT

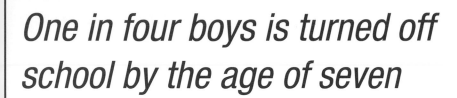

One in four boys is turned off school by the age of seven

Almost one in four boys in the UK is already 'anti-school' by the age of seven, a major survey has revealed.

Boys of this age are more than twice as likely as girls to say they do not like school, according to a study from the Institute of Education, University of London. 24% do not enjoy primary school, compared with only 10% of girls.

The research, which involved more than 14,000 children, also found that 63% of seven-year-old girls, but only 43% of boys, like school 'a lot'.

The findings have emerged from the *Millennium Cohort Study*, which is tracking the development of children born in England, Scotland, Wales and Northern Ireland between 2000 and 2002. The study's latest survey, carried out in 2008/09, has confirmed that seven-year-old boys are much less keen than girls on reading. Less than half of the boys (48%) said they enjoy reading, compared with nearly two-thirds of girls (65%).

63% of seven-year-old girls, but only 43% of boys, like school 'a lot'

Boys appear to like number work and science marginally more than girls do. However, girls of this age appear to be more focused on their schoolwork and are more likely than boys to say they always try their best at school.

Four in five girls also say they behave well in class – a claim made by only three in five boys. Half of the girls (51%) believe that their teachers think they are clever, compared with 44% of the boys.

The researchers who analysed the children's responses, Aleks Collingwood and Nadine Simmonds, of the National Centre for Social Research, also point out that girls seem to be happier, in general, than boys. Boys are more likely to say they are worried or admit they have short tempers.

The survey also found that boys enjoy:

⇨ watching television, videos and DVDs more than girls do (boys 79%: girls 68%);

⇨ playing console games such as Xbox and PlayStation (boys 82%: girls 52%);

⇨ taking part in sports and outdoor games (boys 74%: girls 66%).

However, girls are more likely than boys to say they like:

⇨ listening to, and playing, music (girls 66%: boys 46%);

⇨ drawing and making things (girls 81%: boys 62%).

The findings appear in a report published today by the Institute of Education's Centre for Longitudinal Studies: *Millennium Cohort Study, Fourth Survey: A User's Guide to Initial Findings*. Copies of the report can be downloaded from www.cls.ioe.ac.uk/MCSFindings.

15 October 2010

⇨ The above information is reprinted with kind permission from the Centre for Longitudinal Studies, Institute of Education, University of London. Visit www.ioe.ac.uk for more information.

© *Institute of Education*

One way to make studying more interesting...

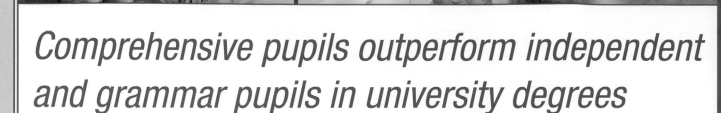

Comprehensive pupils outperform independent and grammar pupils in university degrees

Information from the Sutton Trust.

Students from comprehensive schools are likely to achieve higher-class degrees at university than independent and grammar school students with similar A-level and GCSE results, a major study commissioned by the Sutton Trust and the Government shows. This is one of the main findings from a five-year study by the National Foundation for Educational Research tracking 8,000 A-level students to investigate whether the US-based SAT could be used in university admissions in the UK.

A comprehensive school student with A-level grades BBB, for example, is likely to perform as well in their university degree as an independent or grammar school student with A-level grades ABB or AAB – i.e. one to two grades higher. Comprehensive school pupils also performed better than their similarly qualified independent and grammar school counterparts in degrees from the most academically selective universities and across all degree classes, awarded to graduates in 2009.

> *A comprehensive school student with A-level grades BBB ... is likely to perform as well in their university degree as an independent or grammar school student with A-level grades ABB or AAB*

The final report from the study published today concludes that the SAT results are a poorer predictor of degree results than A-levels or GCSEs, and that the test does not identify academic potential among disadvantaged pupils that might be missed by A-levels.

Sir Peter Lampl, chairman of the Sutton Trust, said: 'These findings provide further evidence that universities are right to take into account the educational context of students when deciding whom to admit – alongside other information on their achievements and potential.

'We are obviously disappointed that the SAT does not provide an extra tool in helping to identify academic talent among students from less privileged homes – but this study does at least demonstrate the need for all university admissions tests to be properly evaluated in this way. One issue has been that during the last five years the SAT has become less of an aptitude test and more of an achievement test similar to A-levels.'

The study found that comprehensive school students, who achieve the same level of degree as students from an independent or grammar school (with the same GCSE attainment and other background characteristics), are likely to have an average A-level grade that is approximately 0.5 to 0.7 of a grade lower.

These differences emerge for all types of universities, including the most academically selective universities – despite the fact that a greater proportion of grammar and independent school pupils end up at these institutions. The study took into account the fact that some universities demand higher A-level grades for entry than others. The final report focuses on the degree results of 2,750 students who graduated in 2009.

The study concludes that the SAT has some power to predict degree outcomes but it does not add any additional information, over and above that provided by GCSEs and A-levels (or GCSEs alone), at a significantly useful level. It finds no evidence that the SAT provides sufficient information to identify students with the potential to benefit from higher education whose ability is not adequately reflected in their A-levels or GCSEs. Meanwhile the SAT was found not to distinguish between the most able university applicants, for example those who get three or more A grades at A-level.

Notes

This is the final report of a five-year research study, co-funded by the Department for Business, Innovation and Skills (BIS), the National Foundation for Educational Research (NFER), the Sutton Trust and the College Board, examining the validity of an aptitude test (the SAT) for use in higher education (HE) admissions.

The study aimed to provide information on:

⇨ how the SAT could help predict university outcomes together with A-levels;

⇨ whether the SAT could distinguish between the most able students who get straight As at A-level;

⇨ if the SAT could help identify students from disadvantaged backgrounds who may have the potential to benefit from higher education.

3 December 2010

⇨ The above information is reprinted with kind permission from the Sutton Trust. Visit www.suttontrust.com for more information.

© Sutton Trust

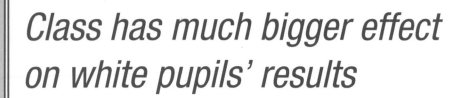

Class has much bigger effect on white pupils' results

Poverty has a much greater influence on how White British pupils do at school than it does on the academic performance of other ethnic groups, two new studies have concluded.

Researchers investigating academic performance in an inner London borough found that, for pupils from most ethnic minorities, the socio-economic backgrounds of each child's parents had only limited impact on how much progress they made during the last four years of primary school.

While White British pupils from well-off families were the top-performing ethnic group at age 11, those eligible for free school meals had among the worst results

However, for White British pupils, the picture was very different, with those from better-off homes pulling away dramatically from their peers from less advantaged backgrounds. This meant that, while White British pupils from well-off families were the top-performing ethnic group at age 11, those eligible for free school meals (FSM) had among the worst results.

Professor Steve Strand, of the University of Warwick, will present the findings at the British Educational Research Association's conference in Warwick today (3 September 2010). They come from an investigation into pupil performance in the ethnically diverse south London borough of Lambeth, commissioned by the borough council itself.

Professor Strand says: 'The effects of economic disadvantage are much less pronounced for most minority ethnic groups. Those from low socio-economic backgrounds seem to be much more resilient to the impact of disadvantage than their White British peers.'

The findings are consistent with a new national study, being presented at BERA on Saturday, 4 September. This shows that there is a bigger gap between the GCSE performance of pupils from disadvantaged and non-disadvantaged backgrounds among white teenagers than for any other ethnic group among those categorised.

Some 31 per cent of white pupils eligible for free school meals (FSM) achieved five A*-C GCSE grades, the study found, compared to 63 per cent among those from better-off backgrounds who were not eligible for FSM. This performance gap of 32 percentage points was much higher than that of any of the other six ethnic groups; for Bangladeshi teenagers, it was only seven points, and for Chinese pupils, only five points.

This second study, by academics at the Institute of Education and Queen Mary, University of London, also found greater differences in the academic performance of middle- and working-class white pupils, as defined by their parents' occupations, than was the case for other ethnic groups.

Some 31 per cent of white pupils eligible for free school meals (FSM) achieved five A*-C GCSE grades

The research reveals a recent improvement in the performance of Bangladeshi pupils – especially girls – but found that Black Caribbean pupils had the worst results overall, with the performance of Caribbean boys 'of particular concern'.

Professor Ramesh Kapadia, of the Institute of Education, who led the study, says: 'There are many minority ethnic groups who perform better at GCSE than the white population and, for those who perform less well, the evidence suggests this is linked to social class much more than to ethnicity.'

Establishing why the social class gap is so much bigger for White British pupils than others is not easy. However, Professor Strand says it is likely that White British pupils from well-off families have better access to 'social and economic capital' than their counterparts from other ethnic groups, and that white working class parents might have, on average, lower educational aspirations for their children than those from immigrant groups.

He says: 'White families of high socio-economic status have more resources to be able to invest in education, such as buying tutors for their children, and they might be a bit more savvy about ensuring that their children go to schools with similar pupils and good results. In terms of families of low socio-economic status, more recent immigrant groups such as the Portuguese, Pakistani and Bangladeshi communities often see education as the way out of the poverty they have come from.

White working class parents might have, on average, lower educational aspirations for their children than those from immigrant groups

'By contrast, if you've been in a white working class family for three generations, with high unemployment, you don't necessarily believe that education is going to change that. All of these factors may combine to make the effect of socio-economic status remarkably strong for White British kids.'

Professor Kapadia says: 'A new finding from our research is that African and Bangladeshi girls have improved their performance markedly at GCSE in the last few years. This may be linked to cultural aspirations and expectations, as well as parental support for education – as appears to have been the case for Indian and Chinese pupils for many years.'

Disadvantage, ethnicity, gender and educational attainment: The case of White working class pupils will be presented by Steve Strand at the BERA conference today (3 September).

Ethnicity and class: GCSE performance, will be presented by Ramesh Kapadia at BERA tomorrow (4 September).

3 September 2010

⇨ The above information is reprinted with kind permission from the British Educational Research Association. Visit their website at www.bera.ac.uk for more information.

© British Educational Research Association

Educational attainment at 16 by ethnic group, 2009/10, England
Percentage of students at the end of KS4 without five or more GCSEs (or vocational equivalent)

■ In receipt of free school meals   ▨ Not in receipt of free school meals

Ethnic group	In receipt of FSM	Not in receipt of FSM
Bangladeshi	4%	4%
Black African	6%	3%
Black Caribbean	8%	5%
Indian	3%	2%
Pakistani	7%	4%
White British	16%	4%
White other	12%	7%

Source: National Pupil Database, Dept. for Education (Crown copyright). Figures taken from the graph UK Educational attainment at age 16, Guy Palmer, The Poverty Site, www.poverty.org.uk

BRITISH EDUCATIONAL RESEARCH ASSOCIATION

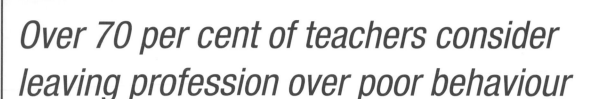

Over 70 per cent of teachers consider leaving profession over poor behaviour

Information from Teacher Support Network.

More than 70 per cent of teachers have considered quitting teaching as a result of poor behaviour in schools, a new survey will reveal tomorrow (Monday). 92 per cent of teachers, who responded to the 2010 Behaviour Survey from Teacher Support Network, Parentline Plus and the National Union of Teachers (NUT) said that student behaviour had got worse over the course of their career, which had led many to think about changing professions.

'It is with deep sadness that after 16 years as a teacher that I will now be leaving the profession,' said Joules, in a post to Teacher Support Network's online forum on behaviour. 'This is due to stress and depression caused by several physically and verbally abusive incidents by students. (…) I am not prepared to (…) damage my health any further.'

The online survey of teachers also found that, like Joules, 81 per cent of respondents had experienced stress, anxiety or depression as a result of bad behaviour, while 79 per cent of teachers said that they felt unable to teach as effectively due to poor behaviour.

92 per cent of teachers said that student behaviour had got worse over the course of their career

'We know from the marked increase in the use of our behaviour-related services over the last year, that poor behaviour is at the heart of many of teachers' health and wellbeing issues,' said Julian Stanley, Chief Executive of Teacher Support Network. 'We are not saying that behaviour is an issue in every classroom, in every school, but we are concerned that poor behaviour is leading some great teachers to leave the profession. Parents and teachers need to work together to create safe, respectful school communities, where teachers, and by extension their children, can reach their full potential.'

The survey, which will be the focus of a Conservative Party Breakfast Fringe event tomorrow morning, held by Teacher Support Network and Parentline Plus with the Minister of State for Schools Nick Gibb MP, revealed that teachers were in favour of extending disciplinary powers for teachers set out by the Government in July, although interestingly 81 per cent of respondents did say that they had never used existing search powers.

A further 95 per cent of teachers involved in the survey said that guidance for parents about their responsibilities to support school behaviour policies was essential or important to improving student behaviour in the future. More collaboration between parents and teachers was welcomed with policies such as annual reviews of school behaviour involving all staff, parents and students, and School Improvement Plans that consider staff concerns, seen as essential.

79 per cent of teachers said that they felt unable to teach as effectively due to poor behaviour

'The results of this survey make worrying reading. It is vital that schools work with parents to engage them and ensure they understand their important role in their child's education, including reinforcing the school's messages about acceptable behaviour' said Jeremy Todd, Chief Executive of Parentline Plus. 'For many parents the school environment can be an intimidating one, perhaps reminding them of their own unpleasant school experiences. It is important that schools reach out to those parents who do not feel comfortable in a number of schools working to help those families whose children display challenging behaviour in the classroom. Simple techniques and confidence building in parents whose children are not able to behave in class can be very effective and enable children to stay in the classroom and behave, preventing them from permanent exclusion.'

Christine Blower, General Secretary of the NUT, the largest teaching union, said: 'The survey clearly shows that teachers see the sharing of best practice across schools both locally and nationally as being the best way forward to deal with student behaviour issues. The introduction of the academies and free schools programme could see much of this valuable work jeopardised. Central specialist services play a valuable role in providing both support and training for teachers. Government spending cuts threaten the existence of such teams.'

3 October 2010

⇨ The above information is reprinted with kind permission from Teacher Support Network. Visit www.teachersupport.info for more information.

TEACHER SUPPORT NETWORK

Major assaults on staff reach five-year high

Last year, 44 had to be rushed to hospital with serious injuries.

By Kerra Maddern

Almost 300 school staff have suffered 'major' injuries in the past ten years as a consequence of violent attacks so severe that they have had to leave in an ambulance, new Government figures show.

A total of 44 were so seriously hurt in the last academic year that they had to be rushed to hospital – the highest number in more than five years. Over the same period, 207 more teachers were assaulted and needed longer than three days to recover.

The statistics, revealed by Schools Minister Nick Gibb in answer to a parliamentary question this week, show that 2,126 teachers have been violently injured at school since 2001. A total of 17,120 pupils have been suspended for assaulting an adult in school in 2008/09.

In a recent survey this year, 38 per cent of members of teaching union ATL said they had had to 'deal' with physical aggression, and 7.6 per cent said they had suffered 'physical harm'.

A teacher on the *TES* forums, writing under the name Darjones, said his school had not done enough for him following an assault. 'I've had very little support or no support at all (after being shot at by a pupil with a ball-bearing gun). There seems to be a loop in the law system and I didn't get any representation in court.

'The boy got off with nothing and the papers were allowed to report on the boys' views, while I couldn't defend myself. I thought perhaps I couldn't be the only teacher in the UK who has had a gun pointed at their head and fired.'

Julian Stanley, chief executive of the Teacher Support Network, said: 'We believe that great teachers are made in part by the environment in which they work.

'How can we expect teachers to reach their full potential or, by extension, our children to reach theirs if teachers are not fully protected and supported?

'When violence and disruption occurs in schools, it can have a negative effect on both the wellbeing of teachers and the attainment of pupils.

'Training is vitally important to ensure that they can manage violence and disruption confidently and effectively and should be provided to every teacher.'

Mary Bousted, chief executive of ATL, said: 'Regrettably, we are not surprised by these statistics. Every year some staff suffer violence from pupils and some are so severely affected they aren't able to continue working in schools.

'Any violence against education staff is unacceptable. Schools need to be safe places where pupils and staff alike feel safe from harm and can work in a calm environment.'

Education Secretary Michael Gove is expected to announce changes to school discipline laws in the forthcoming White Paper.

A Department for Education spokeswoman said: 'Violence against teachers is completely unacceptable – that's why we are sweeping away red tape and giving schools the tough powers they need to get a grip in the classroom.'

At present, the only official national record of assaults against teachers is held by the Health and Safety Executive, which records significant injuries reported to it.

The Government still does not collect detailed information about assaults in school – something teaching unions have campaigned for.

19 November 2010

⇨ The above information is reprinted with kind permission from the *Times Educational Supplement*. Visit www.tes.co.uk for more information.

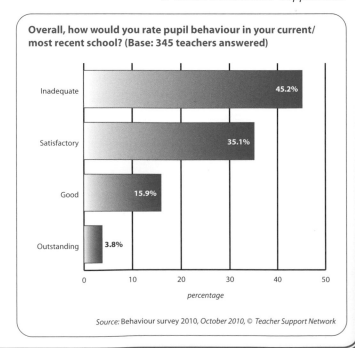

Overall, how would you rate pupil behaviour in your current/ most recent school? (Base: 345 teachers answered)

- Inadequate — 45.2%
- Satisfactory — 35.1%
- Good — 15.9%
- Outstanding — 3.8%

percentage

Source: Behaviour survey 2010, October 2010, © Teacher Support Network

TIMES EDUCATIONAL SUPPLEMENT

Maintenance allowance axed in £500 million budget raid

Chancellor seizes funds to finance plans to raise participation age to 18 by 2015.

Education maintenance allowance (EMA) will be scrapped in order to fund the compulsory education and training of all under-19s.

A replacement programme of targeted support for those most in need is likely to have a budget just a fraction of the size of EMA, as the Government seeks to save £500 million of the total £574 million budget.

George Osborne, the Chancellor, told the House of Commons: 'We will fund an increase in places for 16- to 19-year-olds, and raise the participation age to 18 by the end of the Parliament – and that enables us to replace education maintenance allowances with more targeted support.'

The Department for Education justified the decision by saying that evaluations of the allowance showed that 90 per cent of the money was 'dead weight', going to students who would have attended anyway.

But an Institute for Fiscal Studies report said EMA was a significant factor in improving staying-on rates in education, particularly for boys and for the poorest students. It said it had boosted participation by around six percentage points.

Child benefit for 16- to 18-year-olds, which is also claimed by parents wealthier than EMA claimants, is to be retained at a cost of £1.8 billion.

It is also not clear if the £500 million saving will be enough to fund full participation by under-19s by 2015, as the Government has promised. The former Department for Children, Schools and Families estimated the cost would be £774 million, while Professor Alison Wolf, now recruited by the Government to review vocational education, estimated that the real figure could be double that, at £1.5 billion.

While the total budget for 16-to-19 education will increase in real terms, increased participation will cause the funding per student to fall, the Chancellor admitted.

The Association of Colleges (AoC) has called on the Government to protect its members' budgets and reduce the higher rate of funding for schools first.

A source in the Department for Education said they were 'sympathetic' but no decision had yet been made about how to implement lower rates of funding, or modelling carried out on the impact for individual schools and colleges.

Colleges are particularly concerned about EMAs because they teach 69 per cent of students receiving support. In some, such as Joseph Chamberlain Sixth Form College in Birmingham, more than three quarters of students come from families earning under about £20,000, and are eligible for the maximum grant.

Julian Gravatt, assistant chief executive of the AoC, said that tackling inefficient small school sixth forms and levelling funding between schools and colleges could save £250 million.

He said: 'We are concerned about the prospects of students from poorer families following the announcement of the withdrawal of the educational maintenance allowance and would like to see more detail about what is meant by "more targeted support" for these young people.

'The Association of Colleges suggests the Government should protect education maintenance allowances for young people from the most disadvantaged backgrounds by tackling inefficiency in small school sixth forms and closing the funding gap between schools and colleges.'

Sally Hunt, general secretary of the University and College Union, said: 'We are appalled to learn that education maintenance allowances are at risk. The simple message here seems to be: "Don't be poor".'

22 October 2010

⇨ The above information is reprinted with kind permission from the _Times Educational Supplement_. Visit www.tes.co.uk for more information.

TIMES EDUCATIONAL SUPPLEMENT

Will White Paper help poorest pupils do better?

Information from Save the Children.

The Government has announced an overhaul to the education system in its White Paper. While we support the proposed changes meant to encourage social mobility, we're disappointed the pupil premium isn't accompanied by increases to schools' funding.

The Education Secretary, Michael Gove, has outlined plans in the White Paper called *The importance of teaching* to transform teacher training and recruitment in order to put teachers at the heart of school improvement, focus more on children's performance in academic subjects, and make it easier to remove poor teachers and exclude disruptive children.

The pupil premium isn't accompanied by increases to schools' funding

One of the proposals is to raise the threshold at which schools are considered to be 'failing' to fewer than 35% of pupils achieving five GCSEs graded A to C. Schools will be ranked higher for the number of pupils taking GCSEs in five core subjects – English, maths, science, a language, and a humanities' subject. And a new 'English Baccalaureate' will be introduced to reward pupils studying traditional subjects to a high standard.

Pupil premium: will it deliver?

Under the proposals, head teachers in England will receive around £2,400 more per year for every poor pupil enrolled at their school. The money is designed to encourage the best schools to recruit more children eligible for free meals amid fears they perform much worse than other pupils.

'There's been much about returning to traditional teaching in schools today: one of the oldest traditions in British schooling is that poorest pupils do far less well than their better-off friends,' said Sally Copley.

'It's a scar on our society that more boys from Eton get three As at A-level than all the poorest boys in the state system put together. So we support moves to get top-quality teachers into challenging schools, proposals to ensure poorer pupils get into outstanding schools and more accountability on these children's progress. Yet amidst all Michael Gove's promises on social mobility we're disappointed that the long-awaited pupil premium – £2.5 billion meant to be spent on the poorest pupils – doesn't come on top of a real terms' increase in schools funding. The danger is, it will be used to plug shortfalls in overall school budgets,' Copley continued.

25 November 2010

⇨ The above information is reprinted with kind permission from Save the Children. Visit www.savethechildren.org.uk for more information.

Is the EMA really a handout above criticism?

Reforming the Education Maintenance Allowance would not be a straightforward attack on the poor.

By Deborah Orr

Blind acceptance that all benefits are good is not healthy, especially when the issue is so controversial. Take the Education Maintenance Allowance. There are those who defend it absolutely, just as it is. Yet round my way, one teenage child of a barrister receives it (the mother and father live apart), and one teenage grandchild of a distinguished journalist receives it, while attending a private school paid for by the grandparent.

Even without such anomalous use of a well-meaning system, there is surely room for criticism. I don't think Beveridge would be impressed to learn that further education was now something young people had to be paid to do, especially when their parents were still receiving benefits to support and house them. It's a bit sad when school is so little valued, and also something of a poor indictment of what went on during the previous 11 years of education.

So, something worth discussing at least, rather than totally dismissing as nothing but a straightforwardly ideological attack on the poor. Some reform? Some devolution to the schools themselves? Surely EMA can't be the one perfect thing in an otherwise imperfect world?

20 January 2011

Free schools

Information from the Department for Education.

The Secretary of State for Education, the Rt Hon Michael Gove, has unveiled the major first step towards free schools by inviting groups interested in setting up a new school to come forward and start developing their proposals.

Free schools are all-ability, state-funded schools, set up in response to parental demand. The most important element of a great education is the quality of teaching and free schools will enable excellent teachers to create schools and improve standards for all children, regardless of their background.

Ministers are working right across Government to remove red tape which can prevent new schools from setting up, ranging from planning laws to the Department's own school premises rules.

Free schools are all-ability, state-funded schools, set up in response to parental demand. Free schools will enable excellent teachers to create schools

For those interested in having a new school in their area, but without the time or experience to set one up, there will be advice available from the New Schools Network, an independent charity. The New Schools Network can also link them with more experienced groups and other parents to help make a new school a reality.

As part of this process announced by ministers, the Department will work with a range of different groups who want to join this first wave of free schools. By working with these early groups, the Department will support them to iron out any difficulties they face, and develop the models for the development of future free schools. We expect the first of these schools to be able to open in September 2011.

These new schools will be academies, which are publicly-funded independent schools, free from local authority control. They will enjoy the same freedoms as traditional academies, which include setting their own pay and conditions for staff, freedom from following the National Curriculum and the ability to change the lengths of their terms and school days. All free schools will be accountable like other state schools via inspections and tests.

Any groups interested in establishing a new free school may contact the New Schools Network to discuss their ideas before filling out a proposal form. You can download the full letter from the Department to the New Schools Network from the associated resources on the Department for Education's website.

These new schools will be academies, which are publicly-funded independent schools, free from local authority control

The Secretary of State for Education has also written to all local authorities setting out the Department's new policy on free schools.
28 October 2010

⇨ The above information is reprinted with kind permission from the Department for Education. Visit www.education.gov.uk for more information.

FREE SCHOOL IS **YOUR SCHOOL**
Proudly sponsored by *Fizzy Cola*

DEPARTMENT FOR EDUCATION

The truth about free schools

Information from NASUWT, The Teachers' Union.

Definition in statute

The provision for free schools was introduced in the Academies Act 2010. Section 9 of the Act refers to additional schools, i.e. schools that do not replace a maintained, foundation, trust, voluntary-aided or voluntary-controlled school. An academy would always replace one of these types of school. These additional schools are the so-called free schools.

The Department for Education (DfE) says that free schools may be set up by a wide range of proposers – including charities, universities, businesses, educational groups, teachers and groups of parents – in response to parental demand, to improve choice and drive up standards for all young people, regardless of their background. The DfE says that free schools will provide an inclusive education to young people of all abilities, from all backgrounds, and will be clearly accountable for the outcomes they deliver.

The schools will have placed upon them the same legal requirements as academies and have the same freedoms and flexibilities. The freedoms include:

⇨ the ability to set their own pay and conditions for all staff from the outset;

⇨ greater control of their budget;

⇨ freedom from following the National Curriculum;

⇨ freedom to change the length of terms and school days;

⇨ freedom from local authority control.

The DfE asserts that, like academies, free schools will be funded on a comparable basis to other state-funded schools and will not be profit making.

Background and international comparisons

The free school model is based on a similar scheme in Sweden.

Whilst the Coalition Government in the UK is continuing to promote the Swedish model, serious concerns are being raised in Sweden about its educational effectiveness.

Per Thulberg, Director General of the Swedish National Agency for Education, Skolverket, has said: 'This competition between schools that was one of the reasons for introducing the new [free] schools has not led to better results.'

In instances in Sweden where a free school had improved its results, it is now recognised that this is as a result of the selection of pupils with 'better backgrounds' than those who attended the institutions the free schools had replaced.

A report by the Swedish National Agency for Education in 2004 found that, far from improving the life chances of the poorest in society, free schools practise social segregation.

In promoting the free and academy school models, the Coalition Government often also references the Charter Schools in the USA. Michael Gove, the Secretary of State for Education, has suggested that the USA model of Charter Schools, and specifically the Knowledge is Power Program (KIPP) schools, could be replicated in the UK.

95% of the public are opposed to schools being run by private companies, voluntary organisations, charities and universities

The Charter School Movement has faced serious criticisms by influential thinkers and academics on the grounds that:

⇨ the results are not any better than other state schools;

⇨ they are not effective for low-performing students;

⇨ they have very poor rates of completion, particularly for students from the poorest communities;

⇨ they are unstable institutions – of the 5,250 Charter Schools opened in the USA up to August 2010, one in eight had already closed;

⇨ teachers face greater workloads and are dissatisfied with their working conditions;

⇨ teacher turnover is much higher than in other schools;

⇨ experienced teachers are paid less.

The facts about free schools

Free schools are state-funded independent schools. They will exercise the same freedoms as academies. In free schools there is no automatic recognition of trade unions.

NASUWT

They will be inspected by Ofsted and will be bound by the Admissions Code and be part of the local admissions arrangements. The DfE says that it will set clear expectations around the results and outcomes free schools are expected to achieve and they will be held accountable against those expectations.

There are no restrictions on who can open a free school and there is no statutory requirement to consult the local authority, parents or the local community. It is for the proposer to consult who they consider appropriate. It is only necessary for the Secretary of State to take into account what the impact of establishing the additional school would be likely to be on maintained schools, academies and institutions within the further education sector in the area in which the free school is, or is proposed to be.

The Coalition Government's stated aim is to make it easier for groups of parents, charities, universities, businesses, educational groups, teachers and others to set up their own free school. Encouragement was given in the Conservative election manifesto, in particular to parents where local authorities were seeking to reorganise school provision.

There are a number of private sector organisations looking to offer their services to parents and teachers to run the free schools for profit.

The public's view of free schools

There is no evidence of public clamour for free schools or for the involvement of more providers of schools in the state sector. Research conducted by Ipsos MORI in 2010 found that parents and the public rate highly the quality of state schools and believe that such provision should be directly linked to local authorities.

According to the Ipsos MORI survey findings, 95% of the public are opposed to schools being run by private companies, voluntary organisations, charities and universities; 96% of the public were not supportive of the concept of parent-led (free) schools. In both of these areas, the public response is underpinned by a desire for local, democratically-accountable schools.

⇨ The above information is reprinted with kind permission from NASUWT, The Teachers' Union. Visit www.nasuwt.org.uk for more information.

© NASUWT, The Teachers' Union

Research shows that most parents are happy with schools

Information from Research and Information on State Education (RISE).

A research review published today by RISE (Research and Information on State Education) shows conclusively that, when asked in detailed surveys, the overwhelming majority of parents are satisfied with their children's schools.

The publication of this review is timely in view of the attention currently being paid to the possibility that parents who are dissatisfied with local school provision might start their own schools.

The overwhelming majority of parents are satisfied with their children's schools

The review analyses surveys of parents' opinions about their children's schools over the past five years. The analysis also reveals that, despite the emphasis placed on academic results by policy makers, the research contains much evidence to suggest that they are not as important to most parents as is often assumed.

Parents frequently say that they value factors such as good discipline, the happiness of their child and good communication between school and home more than

exam results. Ease of communication with the school and the provision of clear, accessible and regular information about their child's progress is a priority for many parents.

Surveys also show that many parents are keen to be increasingly involved in school life and in supporting their children's education outside school. They would welcome guidance from schools on how to achieve this.

The review is wide-ranging and includes parents' views on communication, SEN, admissions, attainment and testing.

Margaret Tulloch, a Trustee of RISE, said: 'The Trustees' aim in producing this review was to provide an accessible analysis of what parents say about their children's schools. We hope it will help inform the debate at this important time of change in education.'

9 June 2010

⇨ The above information is reprinted with kind permission from Research and Information on State Education (RISE). Visit www.risetrust.org.uk for more.

© RISE

NASUWT THE TEACHERS' UNION / RISE

Maintained faith schools

Information from the Department for Education.

The English education system developed in partnership with the mainstream Christian churches, which were involved in education before the state and focused on providing education for the poor. Since 1944, faith communities have been able to apply to set up schools in the state sector in response to demand from parents. Today around a third of maintained schools have a religious character and are popularly known as faith schools. In the publication, *The Coalition: Our programme for government*, this Government sets out its intention for all new academies to follow an inclusive admissions policy. It aims to work with faith groups to enable more faith schools and facilitate inclusive admissions policies in as many of these as possible.

A faith academy is an academy with a faith designation order. Faith academies with a denominational (Church of England, Roman Catholic, etc.) religious designation must provide religious education to all pupils at the academy in accordance with the tenets of the academy's faith as set by its faith body. The majority of such academies will teach an awareness of the tenets of other faiths as part of its religious education (RE) curriculum. Those without a denominational designation will normally follow the locally agreed LA syllabus. Such syllabuses must reflect 'that the religious traditions in Great Britain are, in the main, broadly Christian, whilst taking account of the teaching and practices of the other principal religions represented in Great Britain'.

This is a foundation or voluntary school with a religious character. It has a foundation that holds land on trust for the school – and usually provided the land in the first place – and which appoints governors to the school. In many cases, the land is held on trust for the specific purpose of providing education in accordance with the tenets of a particular faith.

Today around a third of maintained schools have a religious character and are popularly known as faith schools

Decisions on the establishment of maintained faith schools are taken under local decision-making arrangements – either by the local authority or the schools adjudicator, following a statutory process. If proposals are approved, to establish a maintained faith school a further application will need to be lodged with the Secretary of State, who is responsible for designating schools with a religious character.

Maintained faith schools are like all other maintained schools in a number of ways. They:

⇨ should follow the National Curriculum;

⇨ participate in National Curriculum tests and assessments;

⇨ are inspected by Ofsted regularly;

⇨ must follow the School Admissions Code of Practice.

How are they different from maintained schools without a religious character?

In addition to needing to meet all the usual requirements of maintained status, there are some areas where maintained faith schools have additional faith-based freedoms and flexibilities:

Thinking about how you prefer to learn, which of these statements do you agree with?

Key Stage 3 / Key Stage 4

Statement	Key Stage 3	Key Stage 4
I like both learning by listening and reading, and learning by doing projects or making things	48%	48%
I prefer to learn by doing projects or making things	44%	38%
Learning by doing things is more fun than academic learning	40%	34%
I find it easier to remember what I've learned by doing things than what I've learned from books	30%	26%
The way things are taught is as important to me as the actual subject of a course	26%	30%
I prefer to learn by listening and reading	17%	23%
None of these	2%	2%

% 0   10   20   30   40   50

Source: Edge Annual Programme of Stakeholder Surveys: Attitudes to learning, conducted by YouGov on behalf of the Edge Foundation. © Edge Foundation 2010

DEPARTMENT FOR EDUCATION

Staffing

Voluntary-aided (VA) schools may fill all of their teaching staff positions with candidates of the school's particular faith. They may also apply a faith test when appointing support staff if there is a genuine occupational requirement to do so.

Voluntary-controlled (VC) and foundation faith schools are required to reserve up to a fifth of their teaching posts as religious posts. These teachers are specifically appointed to teach religious education. The headteacher can be included in this. These schools may not discriminate in relation to support staff or teachers who are not reserved.

Although faith schools may prioritise applicants who are of the faith of the school, they must admit other applicants

Religious education and collective worship

All maintained schools are required to teach RE and to have daily acts of collective worship. In VA faith schools, the syllabus is decided by the governing body in accordance with the trust deeds of the school. Foundation and VC faith schools follow the locally agreed syllabus but parents of any pupil have the right to request their child receives RE in accordance with the tenets of the faith and the school should provide such RE for these pupils.

Admissions

Although faith schools may prioritise applicants who are of the faith of the school, they must admit other applicants if they cannot fill all of their places with children of the faith. They must ensure their admission arrangements comply with the School Admissions Code of Practice.

Ethos

Faith schools have a faith-based ethos that is written into the school's Instrument of Government.

How many are there?

There are just over 20,000 maintained schools in England of which almost 7,000 are faith schools (source: DfE statistics 2010). Around 68 per cent of maintained faith schools are Church of England schools and 30 per cent are Catholic. All but 58 of the maintained faith schools are associated with the major Christian denominations. The 58 schools are comprised of:

⇨ Jewish (38)

⇨ Muslim (11)

⇨ Sikh (4)

⇨ Greek Orthodox (1)

⇨ Hindu (1)

⇨ Quaker (1)

⇨ Seventh Day Adventist (1)

⇨ United Reform Church (1)

All maintained schools are required to teach RE and to have daily acts of collective worship

The major Christian denominations are:

⇨ Christian (32)

⇨ Church of England (4,598)

⇨ Roman Catholic (2,010)

⇨ Methodist (26)

⇨ United Reform Church (1)

⇨ Joint Christian Faiths (61)

8 February 2011

⇨ The above information is reprinted with kind permission from the Department for Education. Visit www.education.gov.uk for more information.

DEPARTMENT FOR EDUCATION

Faith school admission policies criticised

Faith schools' admissions policies risk favouring the middle classes, the Chief Schools Adjudicator warned in his report yesterday.

Gotta have faith?

Schools Adjudicator Ian Craig said faith schools were skewing their intakes towards the middle classes without realising it by favouring pupils whose parents volunteered at a church, for example. He felt such practices disadvantaged parents who do not have the time to volunteer.

Speaking at the publication of the tribunal's annual report, Craig said: 'We are bothered by the complexity of some faith schools' points systems. We have come across points that benefit white middle-class areas and don't benefit the immigrant children in the community.' He said the issue affected all faith groups, but predominantly Christian schools because these outnumber other faith schools.

'We haven't found schools are deliberately skewing their intake, but our view is that this has been the effect. In some cases the faith schools are measuring parents' commitment to the church over and above the number of times a family attend church. Is it a measure of a parent's Christianity if they are bell-ringers at their church? In working-class areas, there might not be the option to do this.'

Craig also warned that some comprehensive schools were illegally selecting pupils according to their academic ability. Schools with specialisms, such as music or languages, are allowed to select ten per cent of their pupils according to their 'aptitude'. However, the difference between ability and aptitude is not clear, according to Craig.

'You tell me how you can select pupils on their musical aptitude using some sort of test that isn't also testing ability. We have spoken to some of the best brains in the country about this and they don't know how to do this.'

Craig said the number of parents' complaints in the last year had risen to 539 from 399 the previous year. Of these, 387 were about admissions – almost double the 201 last year. He put the rise down to increased 'parental engagement'.

Pupil premium as a solution

Education Secretary Michael Gove said it was absolutely right that every parent should want their child to go to an excellent school, so school admissions will continue to be a controversial and sensitive issue. He pointed to the pupil premium as a solution.

'I am committed to driving up educational standards so all parents have that choice of high-quality schools close to home, which is why we are encouraging providers to set up new schools and turning round under-performing schools. And so no child is disadvantaged because of their background, I am introducing the pupil premium.'

Gove said he also intends to make the school admissions framework, including the School Admissions Code, simpler and fairer. 'I have asked my officials to start speaking with key stakeholders,' he added.

Popularity vs. success

Commenting on Michael Gove's response to the Chief Schools Adjudicator report, NAHT general secretary Russell Hobby said it made sense for popular schools to expand in areas of high demand. 'In fact it makes more sense to allow proven providers to grow than to set up untested new schools,' he says.

'A serious concern is that changes in school size may not always reflect school performance,' Hobby continued. 'For example: aspirational parents might choose to send their children to a "good" school in a nearby affluent area to be with "people like them" rather than the local "outstanding" school which is doing great work in a seriously deprived and troubled community. This weakens the local school's ability to serve its community – as research suggests that a balanced intake is required if schools are to be truly inclusive.

'Until we develop an accountability system that measures schools on the progress that all their children make this will stop greater freedoms leading to improved performance.

'Choice will not guarantee improvement where some parents are unable or unwilling to exercise choice. This means that unfettered expansion may not remove weaker schools, merely make them slightly smaller and less efficient. The result could be schools that are "down but not out" and increased social segregation.

'This is not an argument against allowing great schools to grow (assuming they would want to) but an argument in favour of assessing and regulating the impact of expansion on other schools.'

2 November 2010

⇨ The above information is reprinted with kind permission from Education Executive. Visit www.edexec. co.uk for more information.

The Academies Programme

A press release from the National Audit Office.

The National Audit Office has reported that many academies are performing impressively in delivering the Academies Programme's intended improvements. Most are achieving greater rates of improvement in academic attainment than their predecessor schools.

New legislation and Government plans mean that the Programme is likely to expand significantly in the coming years, giving successful schools greater freedoms as well as tackling underperformance. The NAO warns in today's report that academies' performance to date cannot be assumed to be an accurate predictor of how the model will perform when generalised over many more schools, given that the future number is likely to include schools with a much wider range of attainment, and operating in very different community settings.

Overall, academies have increased the rate of improvement in GCSE results when compared with trends in their predecessor schools. And although still below the national average, the proportion of pupils achieving five or more A*-C GCSEs is improving at a faster rate than in maintained schools with similar intakes. However, a small number of academics have made little progress, particularly when English and mathematics are taken into account.

Overall, academies have increased the rate of improvement in GCSE results when compared with trends in their predecessor schools

The proportion of academy pupils from socially disadvantaged backgrounds has reduced, although it remains over twice the national average, and academies now have higher absolute numbers of these pupils on average than when they first opened. The performance of academy pupils from more challenging circumstances (those who are registered as eligible for free school meals, have English as an additional language or have special educational needs) has improved over time. However, the attainment gap between these pupils and others has grown wider in academies than in maintained schools with similar intakes, since less disadvantaged pupils appear to benefit more immediately from improved standards at the academy.

The rate at which new academies have been opening has increased rapidly in recent years, creating challenges around timely staff restructuring and appointment of senior teams. If not dealt with effectively, these challenges can impact significantly on teaching and learning, financial health and longer-term sustainability. Some academies have found it difficult to achieve financial balance without additional funding. The Department has identified that just over a quarter of academies may require additional financial or managerial support to secure their longer-term financial health, and a significant number have not received the financial contributions originally pledged by their sponsors.

The rate at which new academies have been opening has increased rapidly in recent years

The expansion of the Programme increases the scale of risks to value for money – particularly in the areas of financial sustainability, governance and management capacity. With greater numbers of academies opening in recent years, the Department's capacity to administer and monitor the Programme has been stretched, particularly as funding is administered on an individual basis. Responsibility for administering and monitoring open academies has now transferred to the Young People's Learning Agency, and plans for faster expansion of the Programme will also put pressure on the Agency's resources.

Amyas Morse, head of the National Audit Office, said today:

'Many of the academies established so far are performing impressively in delivering the intended improvements. It cannot be assumed, however, that academies' performance to date is an accurate predictor of how the model will perform when generalised more widely. Existing academies have been primarily about school improvement in deprived areas, while new academies will often be operating in very different educational and social settings.'

10 September 2010

⇨ The above information is reprinted with kind permission from the National Audit Office. Visit www.nao.org.uk for more information.

NATIONAL AUDIT OFFICE

Academies will leave pupils 'unprepared for modern life', say critics

Campaign group argues Coalition's education reforms will lead to inadequate teaching of English, maths and science.

By Jessica Shepherd

Thousands of pupils could leave school with a poor grasp of English, maths and science if key Tory education reforms pass their final stage in the Commons tomorrow, experts have warned*.

The Academies Bill – the Coalition's first major piece of legislation – would allow parents to set up their own schools and pave the way for hundreds more academies.

If, as expected, a majority vote for it, thousands of primary, secondary and special schools could become academies – independent state schools that have opted out of local authority control. This would signal the biggest change to England's school structure since the 1960s.

But an influential campaign group is worried that the Bill removes the requirement for new academies to teach science, maths and English according to the national curriculum.

The Campaign for Science and Engineering warns that this risks leaving students unprepared for modern life.

Imran Khan, the group's director, said it was 'vital that schools teach science and maths to a high standard'. He said: 'Over nine in nine businesses employ people with skills in science, technology, engineering and maths – but two-thirds of all employers report difficulty in recruiting enough of these workers. Not requiring schools to follow the national curriculum for science and maths seriously risks leaving pupils unprepared for modern life.'

Schools Minister Nick Gibb has said he 'trusts teachers to use their professional judgement'. He said: 'They are the people who are best placed to make such decisions. We want more freedom and flexibility for schools, not less.'

Teachers' leaders have criticised the Bill for allowing a school to become an academy without consulting its parents or staff. Christine Blower, general secretary of the National Union of Teachers, said it was 'completely against any common sense understanding of "consultation" for parents to be asked if they want their school to become an academy after the decision has already been taken'.

The original clause of the Bill says: 'Before a maintained school in England is converted into an academy, the school's governing body must consult such persons as they think appropriate. The consultation must be on the question of whether the school should be converted into an academy. The consultation may take place before or after an academy order, or an application for an academy order, has been made in respect of the school.'

Others, including the Conservative chair of the Commons Education Select Committee, Graham Stuart, have attacked the Government for using parliamentary procedures normally reserved for emergency counter-terror laws to rush the bill through before next week's summer recess.

Michael Gove, the Education Secretary, wants the Bill to become law as soon as possible so that schools can become academies as early as September.

Chris Keates, general secretary of the NASUWT union, said the way the Government 'had sought to bludgeon' the bill through was 'arrogant' and 'a disgrace'.

She added: 'It underlines the fact that they are on an ideological mission to demolish state education. The bill is unadulterated Tory policy. Yet the Tories received no mandate from the people of this country to make such a profound change to state education.

'If they had they would have been voted in with a working majority. Instead they are being propped up by a Liberal Democrat leadership who seem to be more concerned to keep seats round the cabinet table than to protect the public interest and the education of children and young people.'

Bob Russell, Lib Dem MP for Colchester, has tabled an amendment to the Bill which would ensure parent governors would be elected to the governing body of an academy, as they are in other state schools. At the moment the bill allows one parent to be appointed to be a governor. His amendment could delay the Bill becoming law if MPs vote on whether to include it.

* The Academies Bill was passed in July 2010 by 317 votes to 225, a government majority of 92.
25 July 2010

THE GUARDIAN

Young people's views on Higher Education

A young people omnibus 2010: a research study among
11- to 16-year-olds on behalf of the Sutton Trust.

Summary

Four in five (80%) young people say they are likely (very + fairly) to go into higher education, the highest level recorded since the survey began in 2003. The proportion of young people who say they are unlikely to go into higher education remains low at 8%, in line with findings from 2008.

A preference for doing something practical (45%) and to begin earning money (45%) remain the primary reasons for not going into higher education, but this year there has been a significant increase in the number of pupils claiming that they are not clever enough (38%), that they won't get good enough exam results (31%), that they don't know enough about it (25%) and that they won't go to university because their parents did not go (21%).

An increase in tuition fees to £5,000 a year would result in around one in six (17%) pupils saying they are unlikely to go into further education, rising to almost half (46%) if fees were raised to £10,000 a year. Those with two working parents would be more likely than average to go into higher education despite tuition fee increases.

Around three in five (62%) young people claim to have some knowledge of the financial help available when going into higher education, though one in five (18%) know nothing at all.

Almost three in five (57%) pupils think that having a degree is the most important factor for getting a well-paid job, regardless of which university it is from. Despite this, seven in ten (71%) express an interest in knowing more about what they could earn in the future with degrees in the same subject but from different universities. With this in mind, three in five (60%) think that if different universities requested varying tuition fees for the same course, it would be worth paying a higher tuition fee if it increased their chances of getting a well-paid job in the future.

One-third of pupils (32%) say they are taught in streams but two in five (42%) say they don't know whether this applies to them, suggesting a lack of familiarity with the term.

Teaching in sets appears to be far more common, with 94% of pupils saying they are taught in set for at least one of their core subjects of maths, English or science, and 64% saying they are taught in sets for all three. Modern Foreign Languages also seem commonly to be taught in sets (50%) but other subjects less so.

One in five (20%) pupils say they have received private or home tuition at some stage – this is most common among those attending schools in London and those from BME backgrounds. In line with previous years, the most common reasons given for receiving private tuition are for help with a specific exam (47%) and general help with school work (41%).

Key findings

Likelihood of going into higher education

Young people's likelihood of going into higher education has increased by seven percentage points since 2008, with four in five (80%) 11- to 16-year-olds now saying they are likely to do this. This increase follows the upward trend largely evident since the research began in 2003, but represents the highest single year-on-year increase to date. This has been caused primarily by an increase of those saying they are fairly likely to go into higher education (41% compared with 34% in 2008).

Just 7% of young people say they are unlikely to go into higher education, with one in ten (11%) unsure either way.

Several demographic factors affect the likelihood of young people going into HE:

⇨ Gender: Once again this year, girls more frequently say they are likely to go into higher education than boys (82% and 77%, respectively). They are also more likely to say they are very likely to go into higher education (42% compared with 36%).

⇨ Year group: Pupils in Years 10 and 11, who are close to making (or have made) their post-compulsory education choices, are more likely than younger pupils in Year 7 to say they will continue into higher education (82% each versus 76%, respectively).

These pupils are also more likely than average to say they are very likely to continue into higher education (45% and 55% versus 27%, respectively). As in previous surveys, Year 7 pupils are most likely to say they are not sure either way yet (15%). However, it is worth noting that Year 7 and Year 8 respondents in this year's survey will be the first cohorts of young people affected by changes to the school leaving age, having to participate in education or training to age 18 (academic year 2015-16) and 17 (academic year 2013-14), respectively, rather than to age 16 as now. There are some signs that this may be having an impact on younger pupils' thoughts about their future. Compared with 2008, for example, there has been a significant, nine percentage point increase in the proportion of Year 8s who say they are likely to go into higher education (as well as a no-significant, three percentage point increase in the proportion of Year 7s who say the same). Whether this is the start of a trend is something that can be tracked during future waves of the study.

⇨ Ethnic origin: Pupils of Black or Asian origin are more likely to say they will go into higher education than white pupils (89% and 90% compared with 79%, respectively).

⇨ Work status of household: Pupils living in households without a working parent are significantly more likely than average to say they will not be continuing into HE (12% compared with 7% on average) and also more likely to say they are unsure about doing so (16% compared with 11%). Those who live in households where two parents or one parent works more frequently say they are likely to continue into higher education than those in non-working households (81%, 80% and 68%, respectively).

⇨ Region: Welsh pupils are more likely than the average (11%) to say they are unlikely to continue into higher education.

⇨ Engagement with school and studying: Perhaps unsurprisingly, pupils who agree that going to university is important in helping people to do well in life are more likely to be planning to go into higher education than those who disagree (84% compared with 68%, respectively). This is also true of those who are positive about all aspects of their schooling including those who feel safe at school, enjoy school activities, learn a lot and believe that they are doing well at school. Those who do not enjoy school and feel they are struggling are less likely to want to continue in higher education.

Reasons for not going into higher education

The most frequently given reasons for not wanting to go into higher education are wanting to do something practical rather than studying from books (45%) and

wanting to start earning money as soon as possible (45%). However, pupils are less likely to state these reasons now than they were in 2008 (52% and 50%, respectively). Compared with 2008, there have been significant increases in several of the other reasons which pupils give for being unlikely to go into higher education, most notably:

⇨ I'm not clever enough (38% up from 22%);

⇨ I won't get good enough exam results to get into university (31% up from 20%);

⇨ I don't know enough about it (25% up from 16%);

⇨ My parents did not go to university (21% up from 6%).

Amongst young people who say they're unlikely to go into HE, girls are significantly more likely than boys to give not being clever enough as a reason for not going into higher education (50% and 28%, respectively).

January-April 2010

⇨ The above information is an extract from the report *A young people omnibus 2010*, carried out by Ipsos MORI on behalf of the Sutton Trust, and is reprinted with permission. Visit www.ipsos-mori.com for more information.

© *Ipsos MORI*

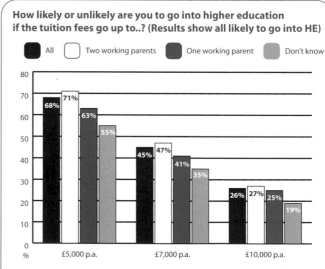

How likely or unlikely are you to go into higher education if the tuition fees go up to..? (Results show all likely to go into HE)

■ All □ Two working parents ■ One working parent ■ Don't know

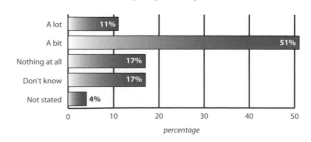

How much, if anything, would you say you know about getting this help with the costs of going into higher education?

Source: A young people omnibus 2010, carried out by Ipsos MORI on behalf of the Sutton Trust © Ipsos MORI

Did you know? Facts about higher education

Information from Universities UK.

The student population is more diverse than you might think

⇨ Two thirds of the student population are mature students.

⇨ While the majority of students are full-time students, more than a third are studying part-time courses.

⇨ There are 64,000 studying medicine or dentistry, and nearly 171,000 training to be nurses.

Student satisfaction with higher education

⇨ More than eight out of ten students said that they were satisfied with their course in the most recent National Students Survey.

Universities give back to the economy

⇨ The higher education sector contributes £31 billion to the UK's Gross Domestic Product, or GDP.

⇨ Universities directly employ 382,000 people throughout the UK.

⇨ Students spend £7.9 billion on living costs, most of which goes into the local economy.

International perspectives

⇨ There is always a lot of talk in the press about there being too many people with degrees, but how do we compare with other countries? Well, although the percentage of adults holding a degree or equivalent qualification has increased from 23% to 33% since 1997, this is still well below the 41% in the United States of America or 49% in Canada.

⇨ Did you know that 16% of all university staff are from overseas and more than 15% of students?

Facts on funding

⇨ No UK student studying full time for an undergrad degree for their first degree has to pay upfront fees.

⇨ Universities have been successful at raising income from other sources. Even during the 2008/09 recession, UK universities managed to raise half a billion pounds in new philanthropic, or charitable gifts.

The percentage of adults holding a degree or equivalent qualification has increased from 23% to 33% since 1997

Supporting and working with employers

Did you know that university course provision heavily involves the input of employers?

⇨ 83% of universities say that they are engaged in collaborative arrangements with employers for bespoke courses.

⇨ Universities also offer programmes that are delivered at the employers' workplace, including foundation degrees and flexible part-time learning.

⇨ Nearly every single university now has a dedicated single enquiry point for small and medium size enterprises (SMEs) and offer specialist facilities such as science parks.

⇨ The above information is reprinted with kind permission from Universities UK. Visit www.universitiesuk.ac.uk for more information.

© Universities UK

Higher education: what will life be like?

Information from Uni4me.

What can the university offer me?

As a student, you will have lots of opportunity to enjoy your spare time, but of course you will have different experiences depending on the size and location of the university, and the course you choose. Each university has different facilities. Most universities have library facilities, social centres, sports facilities and accommodation. Some universities also have shops, clubs and theatres.

If this aspect of your student life is really important to you, be sure to check what the university offers. You can do this by ordering a copy (free of charge) of the latest university prospectus or viewing the facilities online at the university's website.

Living away from home: what are my options?

Your options partly depend on the size and location of the university itself. There is a wide variety of student accommodation of various sizes and types, so you are sure to find a place that will suit you. You will be sent application forms to cover all types of accommodation when your course place is confirmed.

What are halls of residence?

These are special buildings where lots of full-time students live. They usually have single study-bedrooms with shared bathrooms, meeting areas and laundry facilities. Some halls provide most meals, in others you do your own cooking; you choose which you want. First-year students have preference for places in these halls.

If you have a disability, you will find that some places in halls have been adapted to make them accessible. However, the numbers are limited – contact the accommodation office before you apply for a place and they will give you more information on what you should do next.

What about private rentals?

You can make your own arrangements to find a place to live, either with friends or in a place of your own. University accommodation offices have a lot of experience – they will give you advice on what to look out for, and can give you lists of addresses for privately rented rooms, flats or houses. Many students rent a place together as a group, particularly after their first year. You will need to give some money to the landlord as a deposit, which you get back when you leave (as long as the place is left in good condition).

What is the Students' Union?

Every university has a Students' Union, which is run by students for students. You will get discounts for travel, entrance fees to events, museums and galleries. You could also get student discounts in some shops and restaurants, so it is worth becoming a member.

The Students' Union looks after the rights and interests of students, supports you in your studies, and offers facilities to help you enjoy yourself. You will find places to eat and drink and have fun, meeting areas and halls, shops and welfare offices.

The Students' Union is the best place to find out what entertainment is on, or where to go to meet people. There are lots of interested and committed students to help you find your way around.

The Union runs a wide variety of clubs and societies. You can join these when you first start at university, or can find out about them at any other time through the Union. Famous bands often visit big venues at universities, and there are lots of events and trips and activities for all ages of student.

⇨ Information from Uni4me. Please visit www.aimhigher.ac.uk/uni4me for more information.

© Uni4me

UNI4ME

The 2010 university lifestyle survey

Summary of findings from Sodexo.

Since the last survey two years ago, a global recession has caused unemployment in the UK to soar to 2.5 million. Young people have been hit the hardest, and those out of work have found themselves labelled a 'lost generation'.

For many, university is the best place to be, offering shelter from the storm and the chance to boost employment prospects.

But, as our survey shows, it is not an easy ride. Today's students know that a degree in itself is no longer automatically a path into a good job. They feel under growing pressure to do well academically and ensure that, when they come to leave university, they stand out from the crowd. At the same time, financial constraints mean that almost a third are juggling a job alongside their studies, and almost half have day-to-day money worries. Shockingly, nearly one in three has considered dropping out.

It seems that financial and academic pressures mean having fun is lower down the agenda than it once was

The survey also confirms that the traditional student experience is on the wane. Growing numbers are choosing to live at home during their studies, often commuting long distances to attend classes. In new universities, almost a quarter of students never socialise on campus at all, and it seems that financial and academic pressures mean having fun is lower down the agenda than it once was.

From their ambitions, hopes and fears, to how they spend their study time, leisure time and money, the *2010 University Lifestyle Survey* reveals how the UK's 1,272,035 [source: HESA] full-time undergraduate students really live their lives.

Choosing and funding a university education

In previous years, the Sodexo *University Lifestyle Survey* has made it clear that career comes first for today's students. The 2010 results show that this is as much the case as ever during the economic downturn.

Almost three-quarters of this generation of students (73%) are at university in order to enhance their employment prospects and 58% are studying because they think it will increase their earning power.

However, almost as many care about academic factors as about making money. More than half (57%) say they are aiming to improve their knowledge of an area of interest.

The 2010 survey confirms that the recession has had a significant impact on many students' future plans.

More than one in ten (11%) say they have changed career direction or their course as a result of the current economic climate and the tough job market.

Respondents speak of joining university in order to retrain after losing their job, of choosing course options they think will be more attractive to employers, and of abandoning their first choice career due to heightened competition in the area.

'Whilst the economy is like this, I felt it better to stand back, use the time to re-train to put myself in a better position for higher salaries and more job prospects as a graduate in a few years time.' Comments like this might help to explain a surprising finding of this year's survey – the fact that most students still see their debt as an acceptable investment in their future career, despite a big rise in debt levels.

In 2004, under the old fee regime, only 2% of students expected to graduate with more than £20,000 of debt. In 2010, more than a quarter (28%) do. The figure has risen significantly in the last two years too – in 2008, 18% of students expected to graduate owing in excess of £20,000.

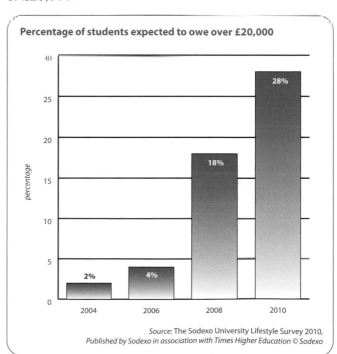

Percentage of students expected to owe over £20,000

Source: The Sodexo University Lifestyle Survey 2010,
Published by Sodexo in association with *Times Higher Education* © Sodexo

SODEXO

Today, exactly half (50%) of students now expect to graduate more than £15,000 in the red. Only 15% of students expect to leave university entirely debt-free.

Nonetheless, the proportion who think their debt is probably or definitely a worthwhile investment in their future has grown slightly, from 64% in 2008 to 67% in 2010.

Student loans are the main source of financial support for students – just over three-quarters (76%) of students have one – but parents are still an important source of income for many, particularly those studying at old universities. Around half of students (49%) rely on their mums and dads for money to help them through university, making parents the second most important source of cash. While just 39% of students at new universities are subsidised by their parents, the figure is 61% for those studying at older institutions.

Student loans are the main source of financial support for students – just over three-quarters (76%) of students have one

A significant number of students also support themselves financially through paid work. Just under a third (31%) of students have a part-time job during term time (down from 33% in 2008), and in new universities, even more students are working during term-time in order to fund their studies.

In modern institutions, 37% juggle studying alongside paid work, against 24% in older universities. Students at old universities are more likely to boost their wallets during the holidays instead, with 27% holding down a part-time job outside term time, against the 20% of students who do so in newer institutions.

For the first time, the survey asked students whether they had considered dropping out of university. Worryingly, almost a third (30%) have considered leaving higher education at some point. The proportion is higher among women than men (32% against 27%), among students in later years of study (34% against 22% in first year), and at new universities (33% against 27% at old). Those who juggle term-time paid work with their studies are also more likely to consider quitting their course (35% against 28% who don't).

Academic pressure is the main reason students cite for considering giving up on their studies. This is a factor for almost half (48%) of students who have considered abandoning university prematurely. Nearly as many (46%) doubt whether they can continue due to financial difficulties. Four in ten (40%) cite poor health, depression or stress, and 35% say they did not like their course.

Lifestyle and eating habits

Cash constraints are forcing students to make changes to their lifestyles.

Nearly six in ten (59%) say they are not going out as often because they need to save money, and almost half (46%) say that, for the same reason, they now go to different venues.

In fact, 56% of students now take cost into account when choosing a venue for a night out – up from 43% in 2008.

While their primary concern in picking a place to socialise is the people who go there, which matters to 57%, this has dropped in importance (down from 63% in 2008) as the emphasis on finding a cheap place to socialise has risen.

Money worries are also impacting on students' eating habits. More than four in ten (42%) have changed their diet in order to cut down their spending. Worryingly, it seems that students think eating healthily costs more money – more than six in ten (63%) who have changed their diet say this means they are eating less nutritious food as a result.

Another shift that could be related to finance is the growing number of students who choose to study while living at home. The proportion living with their parents or family during their time at university has risen from 13% in 2008 to 17%. This is much more likely to be the case among those studying at modern universities, where 23% of students live at home, compared with 10% in traditional universities. However, the most popular type of accommodation, for 38% of students, is still a rented flat or house.

One trend that has continued since the last survey is the high proportion of students who do most of their socialising off campus. In total, 65% of students usually or always meet their friends at non-university venues. In new universities, this is the case for nearly three-quarters (72%) and almost one in four (24%) never socialise at university venues at all.

Socialising was once the biggest event of the day for undergraduates. However, today the majority of students (55%) socialise for a modest two hours or less a day. There is still a small proportion, however (16%) who spend five hours or more on their social lives.

Instead, studying is the most time-consuming activity. More than three quarters (77%) of students spend two to five hours a day in lectures, seminars or lab time and for 18% this takes up more than five hours a day.

Today the majority of students (55%) socialise for a modest two hours or less a day

The issue of contact hours has received considerable media attention, but the majority of students (58%) are happy with the amount of contact time they have with academic staff. As would be expected, however, there are significant differences in satisfaction depending on the number of contact hours students have. While almost three-quarters (73%) with 21 or more contact hours a week would not want more, the figure falls to 50% among students with only one to ten hours of contact a week.

Private study is the second biggest activity, with 71% of students spending between two and five hours a day on this. In 2008, 15% of students put in five hours or more a day and in 2010 the proportion devoting this much time to their studies has risen to 18%.

Students do surprisingly little of their work in the university library. The overwhelming majority (92%) visit the library for no more than ten hours a week. More than six in ten (62%) say they do most of their work in their accommodation instead.

The majority of students have to devote some time every day to travelling, but for some this is a major undertaking, particularly for those who live with their parents or families, more than six in ten of whom (63%) travel for two or more hours every day.

This could be part of the reason why the phenomenon of watching or listening to lectures online is growing. In 2008, just 4% used technology such as podcasts to catch up with lectures in their own time electronically.

The figure that usually listen to lectures remotely, instead of travelling in to attend, has risen to 8% in 2010.

In another online trend, students seem to be getting ever more addicted to social networking sites. The proportion spending 11-20 hours a week communicating with friends via sites like Facebook, Bebo or Myspace has grown from 9% in 2008 to 14%, and of those spending even longer than this from 6% to 11%.

Students do not have regular eating habits. Almost half of them (46%) miss lunch at least once a week and one in ten (10%) never eat breakfast. Dinner is the most regular meal, but 17% of students still skip supper at least once a week. Contrary to popular belief, many of today's students are not regular drinkers either. A quarter of students (23%) do not drink at all, and a further half (49%) drink ten units or fewer a week.

March 2010

⇨ The above information is an extract from Sodexo's report, *University Lifestyle Survey 2010,* and is reprinted with permission. Visit http://uk.sodexo.com for more information.

© Sodexo

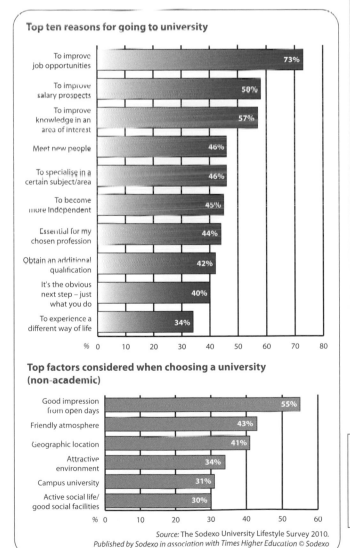

Source: The Sodexo University Lifestyle Survey 2010.
Published by Sodexo in association with Times Higher Education © Sodexo

50% rise in likelihood of England's poorest teenagers going to university since mid-90s

Findings follow report on growing inequalities.

By Jessica Shepherd

Teenagers from the poorest homes in England are 50% more likely to go to university than they were 15 years ago, according to a study that will be welcomed by the Government after other recent reports found that Britain had become a more unequal nation.

The Government-commissioned Hills report, published yesterday, showed inequality is greater than it was in 1980.

Today's study, by the Higher Education Funding Council for England (HEFCE), shows participation rates have soared in the past five years in particular, with disadvantaged 18- and 19-year-olds 30% more likely to enrol at university now than they were in the mid-2000s. But a teenager from the poorest fifth of the population is still much less likely to go to university than one from the richest fifth.

'This report highlights the recent progress we've made in terms of widening participation – which is good news – and how important universities and education are to social mobility,' said Professor Steve Smith, president of Universities UK, the umbrella group for vice-chancellors. 'Although the situation has improved, there is still more that can be done.'

The study attributes the jump in the proportion of disadvantaged young people enrolling at university to Labour's increased funding for schools and drive to widen access to degree courses.

Just one in eight (12.7%) of 18- and 19-year-olds from the poorest homes went to university in the mid-1990s; now almost one in five (19.2%) do. Teenagers from the richest homes have also seen their chances improve – by 15% in 15 years. More than half of teenagers from the richest homes now go to university – 57.3%.

The gap between the richest and poorest teenagers' chances of going to university has widened by 1% over 15 years, although it has narrowed since the mid-2000s.

The HEFCE, which funds universities on behalf of the Government, said its study of 8.8 million teenagers who started a degree between 1994 and this year proves tuition fees have not deterred students from the poorest homes.

A study of social inequality by Professor John Hills of the London School of Economics, published yesterday, found only 4% of children who received free school meals at 15 went on to university, compared with 33% of other children.

HEFCE's study reveals that young men, rich and poor, are going to university in far fewer numbers than young women. Some 270,000 more young men would have needed to go to university since the mid-1990s to match their female counterparts. Young men from the poorest backgrounds have fallen even further behind. In 1994-95, there was only a 1% difference between men and women's participation at university if they were from the poorest homes. Now, there is a 6% gap, with 22% of women going to university compared with 16% of men.

Some 40% of young women from all backgrounds go to university, compared with 32% of young men. This

Main sources of student income

Source	Percentage
Student loans	76%
Parents	49%
Savings	35%
Bursary/scholarship from university	32%
Paid work - part-time job in term-time	31%
Bank overdrafts	30%
Paid work - part-time job in holidays	24%
LEA Grants	19%
Paid work - full-time job in the holidays	13%
Relatives [other than parents]	9%

percentage

Source: The Sodexo University Lifestyle Survey 2010.
Published by Sodexo in association with Times Higher Education © Sodexo

8% difference has grown from a 6% difference in the mid-2000s.

The HEFCE, university leaders and the Government said the rise in poor young people going to university was down to increased funding in schools, improved examination results, a cash incentive for poor teenagers if they stay on at school and a drive by universities to encourage the poorest to apply for degree courses.

But university leaders warned that unless ministers stopped their plan to cut funding to higher education by £950 million, any progress could soon be reversed.

The HEFCE will now analyse the data further to examine the different patterns of university attendance by regions, universities, courses and ethnicity.

John Selby, the HEFCE's director for education and participation, said: 'The results show a substantial increase in the participation rate of those from the most disadvantaged backgrounds. Nevertheless, the participation differences between the most advantaged and the least advantaged, and between women and men, remain very large. There is an awful lot left to do.'

28 January 2010

Fears for 'privatisation' of higher education

Voice, the union for education professionals, has expressed its fears for the future of higher education as the Government publishes its response to Lord Browne's funding review.

General Secretary Philip Parkin said: 'We fear for the future of higher education in this country. Raising fees and withdrawing state funding from many courses will lead to the effective privatisation of university education as graduates shoulder the costs instead of the Government.

'Research has indicated that the fee rises could deter students and we are concerned that students from poorer families in particular will be deterred from attending universities charging higher fees or even from going to university at all.

'Replacing state funding for many courses with income from student fees and "rating" degrees according to graduate employment rates and salaries would demonstrate a truly cynical disregard for the value of education. Those who advocate such schemes know the price of everything but the value of nothing. Liberal Democrat ministers have already abandoned their principles over tuition fees. Politicians, many of whom benefited from a university education before the days of fees and loans, run the risk of pulling up the ladder of opportunity behind them.

'There is already state funding for education at primary and secondary level and it is crucial to continue that into higher education if society values the skills and learning that education brings. We live in a knowledge-based economy and this country needs more graduates.

'In the future, schools may struggle to recruit teachers as more graduates seek the most highly-paid employment, in order to ease their debt burden, rather than socially valuable careers such as teaching.

'As most students already graduate with the burden of large debts and then, on top of loan repayments, have to face increasing costs for housing, pension provision etc. it is unfair that they should have to pay even more.

'Raising the level of fees could make the UK uncompetitive with countries that charge considerably less. Universities could see fewer foreign students and Britain could lose its place as a world centre of excellence in higher education.'

3 November 2010

⇨ The above information is reprinted with kind permission from Voice: the union for education professionals. Visit www.voicetheunion.org.uk for more information.

Millennium mothers want university education for their children

The Millennium generation of UK children may have the most educationally ambitious mothers ever, a new study suggests.

No less than 97% of them want their children to go on to university, even though most did not have a higher education themselves, researchers at the Institute of Education, University of London, have found.

Today, roughly a third of young people in the UK progress from school to higher education. However, that proportion will be much higher in ten years' time if the mothers of children born in the first few years of the new century get their way, a survey of almost 14,000 families has shown.

The Millennium Cohort Study, which is tracking the development of children born in England, Scotland, Wales and Northern Ireland between 2000 and 2002, found that 96% of mothers with the lowest qualifications want their seven-year-olds to go on to higher education. The figure for those with postgraduate qualifications is only slightly higher (98%).

Attendance at parents' evenings is also encouragingly high, say Dr Kirstine Hansen and Dr Elizabeth Jones, who analysed the responses to the study's latest survey. The vast majority of families (93%) had been represented at a parents' evening, and more than half of those who had not attended one said that their school had not yet held such an event.

96% of mothers with the lowest qualifications want their seven-year-olds to go on to higher education

Most parents also told the researchers that they help their child with their reading, writing or maths homework. 85% of parents with either no qualifications or the most basic certificates said they offer such support.

'The overarching impression from the parental interviews is one of all families, right across the social spectrum, taking an interest in the Millennium children's schooling and aspiring for them to do well,' Dr Hansen and Dr Jones say. 'This is a positive sign because previous research has shown that parental involvement and interest in their children's education is a strong predictor of later educational success.'

The study's latest survey, conducted in 2008/09, also found that the average amount of time that seven-year-olds spend on homework is 86 minutes a week. Seven-year-olds in Northern Ireland appear to do most homework (115 minutes per week on average), followed by children in Scotland (87 minutes), England (84 minutes) and Wales (69 minutes).

Most parents also told the researchers that they help their child with their reading, writing or maths homework

In England and Wales it is recommended that children in Years 1 and 2 of primary school should spend one hour a week on homework. In Scotland and Northern Ireland schools are given discretion over homework policy.

15 October 2010

⇨ The above information is reprinted with kind permission from the Centre for Longitudinal Studies, Institute of Education, University of London. Visit www.cls.ioe.ac.uk for more information.

© Centre for Longitudinal Studies

UCAS reports record student applications for university

Tuition fee rise planned for 2012 has caused huge rise in university applications this year.

By Jessica Shepherd

Nearly 600,000 university hopefuls – an all-time record – applied for a place on a degree course this year, official figures showed today.

Applications have risen by 5.1% compared with this time last year, with 583,501 candidates chasing a place this autumn, according to data from the Universities and Colleges Admission Service. UCAS said this was the highest number since it started collecting data in 1964.

The surge has been caused by the likelihood that fees will almost triple for some universities from next year. This year, fees go up to £3,375 a year, but by 2012 universities will be allowed to charge as much as £9,000.

The figures show a dramatic rise in the number of university applications over the last four years. In 2007, there were 402,831 applications.

At least 180,000 applicants are likely to be disappointed, because there are only just over 400,000 places available for undergraduate study each year.

Ministers funded an extra 10,000 places for under-graduates starting at English universities last year amid a dramatic increase in applications, but fierce competition still saw one in three candidates missing out.

The Government will continue to fund an extra 10,000 places this year, but this provision will be withdrawn by 2012.

The figures show a spike in the number of mature students who have applied. Applications from 21-year-olds have grown by 15.3% on last year, while those from 24-year-olds has risen by 11.4%.

The figures give details of applicants' subject choices and show vocational courses are becoming more popular.

There has been an 18% rise in applications for degrees such as medicine and nursing compared with last year, and a 12.8% growth in applications for veterinary science courses. Applications for business-related degrees are up 9.1%.

At the same time, there is a decline in applications for linguistics and classical languages, such as Latin and Greek. Applications for these subjects have dropped by 2.7%.

Women make up 57% of candidates, but the number of men applying is rising slightly faster than the number of women. Men's applications rose by 5.3% compared to last year, while women's increased by 4.9%.

The number of applications from outside the UK rose by 12.5% compared with last year. Some 34,080 non-UK students from within the European Union applied, a rise of 21.6%. Applications from Hong Kong also grew by 17%.

Universities face a financial pinch this year. Funding for teaching will be cut by £300 million, from £4.9 billion to £4.6 billion.

From 2012, universities will be expected to make up the shortfall by charging undergraduates more. Fees rise to £3,375 for students starting this year, but from next autumn universities will be able to charge up to £9,000 a year.

Nicola Dandridge, chief executive of the umbrella group for vice-chancellors, Universities UK, said it was encouraging to see a rise in the popularity of science subjects and in the creative arts, both of which were 'vital for the future growth of the UK economy'.

She urged applicants not to panic at the competition for places. 'There is still a good chance of securing a place at university. It is essential that applicants receive high-quality, targeted information, advice and guidance following the outcome of their applications and should also be sure to apply early for student support.'

It is only when students graduate and earn £21,000 or more that they must repay tuition fees.

David Willetts, the Universities Minister, said the government understood how frustrating it was for young people who wished to go to university but were unable to find a place.

'Going to university has always been a competitive process and not all who apply are accepted,' he said. 'We are opening up other routes into a successful career. Our reforms will make part-time university study more accessible and we are also investing in new apprenticeship places, with an additional 75,000 being created by 2014.'

Les Ebdon, chair of Million, a lobby group for modern universities, said ministers should guarantee a place

THE GUARDIAN

for everyone who was qualified to study for a degree. The alternative was spending money on benefits for people who would have taken degrees but were having to sign on because of a shortage of places, he said.

'In a difficult jobs market, with unemployment on the rise, a degree would vastly improve the life chances of young people who have struggled to find a job after leaving school or college, and it would significantly increase the opportunities of older people who have been made redundant in the recession and are keen to retrain.'

31 January 2011

Ministers push for more apprenticeships

Business Secretary Vince Cable and Skills Minister John Hayes have called on employers to create more apprenticeships to drive economic growth in the UK.

The plea to businesses came as ministers reiterated the Government's plans to increase the funding for apprenticeships to more than £1.4 billion in 2011-12, to mark the start of Apprenticeship Week. Funding for apprenticeships in 2010-11 was just over £1.1 billion.

Cable said: 'I want to reinforce the message to business and young people that apprenticeships are a first-class way to start a career. That is why my department has pledged to work to create some 75,000 additional adult places than those promised by the previous government.

'Some of the most prestigious companies in England – large and small, public and private – employ apprentices and benefit from doing so. More than 30 per cent of Rolls-Royce apprentices have progressed to senior management roles within the company. And 80 per cent of those who employ apprentices agree that they make the workplace more productive. I'm calling on more businesses to follow this lead.'

The Government's skills strategy, published in November 2010, set out reform of the further education and skills system to deliver skills for sustainable growth, with apprenticeships as the central pillar.

Hayes also signalled he wanted to reinforce the shift in how apprenticeships are perceived as he announced that apprenticeship frameworks would be renamed to emphasise the level that has been achieved. For example, Level 2 apprenticeships (GCSE-level equivalent) will now be known as intermediate-level apprenticeships, while Level 3 (A-level equivalent) will become advanced-level apprenticeships and higher apprenticeships will remain unchanged. The UK Commission for Employment and Skills is also working with Sector Skills Councils to develop more higher apprenticeship (Level 4) frameworks.

Hayes said: 'Our ultimate goal remains to see apprentices achieve equivalent esteem and status with university graduates, so that a place on an apprenticeship scheme is as valued as one at a university.'

To reinforce this change in perception, Hayes out-lined his work with the Department for Education and the National Apprenticeship Service to accelerate plans for graduation ceremonies for apprentices, as well as introducing an apprentice honour roll. He said that the two bodies were working together to aid the creation of an alumni network like those used by graduates.

'Apprenticeships are a first-class way to start a career'

Government plans to offer apprenticeship places to people on unemployment benefits are also under discussion, Hayes said.

Sir Michael Rake, BT chairman, said: 'Apprenticeships are undoubtedly good for BT's business and play a key role in ensuring that we maintain and develop a highly skilled workforce. More importantly, for young people, they're a great way to transform their raw enthusiasm into valuable skills that will serve them well wherever their careers take them.'

Major employers that will create a total of more than 12,000 new apprenticeships this year include British Gas, Morrison's, B&Q, BT, McDonald's Restaurants, BAE Systems, Superdrug, Procter & Gamble, Tesco, Nissan and Northgate Managed Services.

7 February 2011

⇨ The above information is from *People Management*, by Claire Churchard on 7 February 2011 and is reprinted with the permission of the publisher, the Chartered Institute of Personnel and Development, London (www.cipd.co.uk).

THE GUARDIAN / CIPD

Economic fears get more adults learning

Economic uncertainty appears to have had a huge impact on the number of adults who are in learning or who are thinking about learning in the future, reports the annual Adult Learners' Week survey, published on Wednesday 13 May 2010.

The proportion of adults who are currently learning, or have done so in the last three years, has risen by four per cent: from 39 per cent in 2009 to 43 per cent in 2010, its highest level for ten years. People in and out of work are reporting record levels of wanting to learn since these surveys started 20 years ago.

The UK-wide survey of nearly 5,000 adults – *A Change for the Better* – from NIACE, also reports that:

⇨ current participation, having fallen to its lowest levels for a decade in 2009, rose by three percentage points to 21 per cent – lower than the highs experienced between 1996 and 2003, but reversing recent reductions;

People in and out of work are reporting record levels of wanting to learn since these surveys started 20 years ago

⇨ women (23 per cent current and 44 per cent current/recent learners) continue to take part in larger numbers than men (20 per cent and 41 per cent, respectively),

⇨ three in five (60 per cent) full-time workers plan to take up learning – a rise of 13 percentage points since 2009; 58 per cent of part-time workers plan to study – a rise of nine percentage points on 2009; and for people seeking work there is a jump of 17 percentage points, with 67 per cent planning to study;

⇨ 56 per cent of ABs, 51 per cent of C1s, 37 per cent of C2s and 30 per cent of DEs report current or recent learning. There are rises of three to four percentage points for ABCs but a jump of six percentage points in DEs is unprecedented. In previous surveys, DEs have never reported more than a single percentage rise, and have always reported within the 24-26 per cent range. Despite this, ABs remain almost twice as likely to participate as DEs;

⇨ the overall numbers planning to study has jumped in 2010 to almost half (47 per cent), the highest number reported in a 20-year sequence of NIACE surveys. Almost as significant is the drop – from 47 per cent in 2009 to 34 per cent in 2010 – who say they are very unlikely to take up learning in the next three years;

⇨ the proportion of people reporting no learning since leaving school has fallen dramatically from 37 per cent in 2009 to 31 per cent in 2010 (marking a total four percentage points below any previous survey) and making clear that the rise in participation is reaching adults previously untouched by adult learning.

Alan Tuckett, Chief Executive of NIACE, said:

'This survey shows something of a sea change in adults' engagement in learning. After years in which the numbers in learning fell overall, and the gulf between the learning rich and the learning poor widened dramatically, there has been a major shift – not only in the proportion of adults who are engaged in learning, but also in adults' expectations of taking part in the near future.

'Perhaps the most striking result in the survey is the first statistically significant improvement in participation by adults from social class DE – the poorest cohort, comprising unemployed people, semi- and unskilled adults and retired people. For 20 years, the percentage of this group reporting current or recent study scarcely shifted, with just one in four participating, whilst more affluent social groups each in turn increased the numbers participating.

The overall numbers planning to study has jumped in 2010 to almost half (47 per cent), the highest number reported in a 20-year sequence of NIACE surveys

'This year's increases can only be just a beginning. If those who benefit least from their initial education are to get a fair share of the opportunities that training and wider learning can bring, this level of increase will need to be emulated in 2011. Yet just to maintain these gains will be challenging, when public finances are under so much pressure. Things may be moving in the right direction, but they have some way to go.'

14 May 2010

⇨ The above information is reprinted with kind permission from NIACE. Visit www.niace.org.uk for more information.

© NIACE

NIACE

KEY FACTS

⇨ In a recent Edge Foundation survey, half of secondary teachers and 39 per cent of parents said their school favoured academic qualifications, with very few saying it favoured vocational ones. (page 1)

⇨ Employers believe many soft skills are better developed by vocational qualifications; these include team working, business and customer awareness, and attitude and enthusiasm. (page 3)

⇨ A study from Cambridge University found that teachers had been forced into a 'tick-list' approach to teaching, which had resulted in pupils being coached to pass exams and tests. (page 5)

⇨ In 2010, 69% of 16-year-olds got five good GCSEs, up from 45% in 1997. (page 7)

⇨ There are at least 771 million illiterate adults worldwide, of whom 64 per cent are women. (page 8)

⇨ There is a bigger gap between the GCSE performance of pupils from disadvantaged and non-disadvantaged backgrounds among white teenagers than for any other ethnic group among those categorised. (page 13)

⇨ In a recent survey of teachers, 81 per cent of respondents had experienced stress, anxiety or depression as a result of bad behaviour, while 79 per cent said that they felt unable to teach as effectively due to poor behaviour. (page 15)

⇨ In a recent survey this year, 38 per cent of members of teaching union ATL said they had had to 'deal' with physical aggression, and 7.6 per cent said they had suffered 'physical harm'. (page 16)

⇨ Free schools are all-ability, state-funded schools, set up in response to parental demand. (page 19)

⇨ The Academies Bill – the Coalition's first major piece of legislation – allows parents to set up their own schools and paves the way for hundreds more academies.

Thousands of primary, secondary and special schools could become academies – independent state schools that have opted out of local authority control. (page 26)

⇨ Four in five (80%) young people say they are likely (very + fairly) to go into higher education, the highest level recorded since 2003. (page 27)

⇨ Students spend £7.9 billion on living costs, most of which goes into the local economy. (page 29)

⇨ Every university has a Students' Union, which is run by students for students. (page 30)

⇨ Almost three-quarters of this generation of students (73%) are at university in order to enhance their employment prospects and 58% are studying because they think it will increase their earning power. (page 31)

⇨ Teenagers from the poorest homes in England are 50% more likely to go to university than they were 15 years ago. (page 34)

⇨ Today, roughly a third of young people in the UK progress from school to higher education. (page 36)

⇨ Nearly 600,000 university hopefuls – an all-time record – applied for a place on a degree course this year. (page 37)

⇨ The Government plans to increase the funding for apprenticeships to more than £1.4 billion in 2011-12. (page 38)

⇨ The proportion of adults who are currently learning, or have done so in the last three years, has risen by four per cent, from 39 per cent in 2009 to 43 per cent in 2010. (page 39)

⇨ The proportion of people reporting no learning since leaving school has fallen dramatically, from 37 per cent in 2009 to 31 per cent in 2010 (page 39)

Academy

Academies (under the Academies Bill 2010) are schools that are state-maintained, but independently run and funded by external sponsors. This gives the school greater freedom from local authority bureaucracy: for example how much they pay their staff and the subjects students are taught. Often, failing state schools are encouraged to apply for academy status.

A-level

An academic qualification taken in England and Wales, generally used to decide Higher Education places. It is usually taken by 16- to 18-year-olds.

Apprenticeship

A form of vocational training which involves learning a trade or skill through working. An apprentice will often shadow an experienced practitioner of a trade, learning the occupation 'on the job'. Some apprenticeships can take many years.

Comprehensive school

Also known as state schools, comprehensive schools are the state-run, Government-funded schools in Britain. Education is free in comprehensive schools.

Free school

Free schools the same freedoms and flexibilities as academies, but they do not normally replace an existing school. Free schools may be set up by a wide range of proposers – including charities, universities, businesses, educational groups, teachers and groups of parents

Further education

Education for 16- to 18-years-olds, for example college or sixth form.

GCSE

This stands for General Certificate of Secondary Education; it is the national exam taken by 16-year-olds in England and Wales. The Scottish equivalent is the Scottish Certificate of Education.

Higher education

Post-18 education, for example university.

Mature student

A student in further or higher education (for example, college or university) who is 21 years old or older at the start of their course.

National Curriculum

The statutory set of guidelines set down by the Government which determine the subject material and attainment targets taught in schools in England and Wales. The National Curriculum applies to pupils up to the age of 16.

Sixth form

Sixth form is a type of post-16 education which enables students to study for their A-levels or equivalents. Some sixth-form institutions are independent colleges, whilst others are attached to secondary schools.

Students' union

Every university has a students' union: an organisation that is run by students, for students. Student unions usually offer a variety of social and sporting opportunities as well as practical services such as help groups and advice centres

UCAS

The Universities and Colleges Admissions Service. This organisation is responsible for organising applications to higher education institutions in the UK. Prospective students do not apply to universities directly, but via UCAS.

Vocational learning

Education that provides practical training for a specific occupation or vocation, for example agriculture, carpentry or beauty therapy. Traditionally this is delivered through 'hands-on' experience rather than academic learning, although there may be a combination of these elements depending on the course.

ACKNOWLEDGEMENTS

The publisher is grateful for permission to reproduce the following material.

Chapter One: School Issues

Attitudes to learning, © Edge Foundation, *Pushy parents turn schools into 'exam factories'*, © Telegraph Media Group Limited 2010, *Study suggests curriculum 'overloaded' and 'narrow'*, © SecEd, *Adapt GCSE to be national exam at 14*, © Sutton Trust, *Are our schools really failing?*, © Fiona Miller, *Education: key facts and figures worldwide*, © Oxfam, *Myth: standards rise is just exams getting easier*, © Times Educational Supplement, *One in four boys is turned off school by the age of seven*, © Institute of Education, *Comprehensive pupils outperform independent and grammar pupils in university degrees*, © Sutton Trust, *Class has much bigger effect on white pupils' results*, © British Educational Research Association, *Over 70 per cent of teachers consider leaving profession over poor behaviour*, © Teacher Support Network, *Major assaults on staff reach five-year high*, © Times Educational Supplement, *Maintenance allowance axed in £500 million budget raid*, © Times Educational Supplement, *Will White Paper help poorest pupils do better?*, © Save the Children, *Is the EMA really a handout above criticism?*, © Guardian News and Media Limited 2010, *Free schools*, © Crown copyright Is reproduced with the permission of Her Majesty's Stationery Office, *The truth about free schools*, © NASUWT, The Teachers' Union, *Research shows that most parents are happy with schools*, © RISE, *Maintained faith schools*, © Crown copyright is reproduced with the permission of Her Majesty's Stationery Office, *Faith school admission policies criticised*, © Education Executive,

The Academies Programme, © National Audit Office, *Academies will leave pupils 'unprepared for modern life', say critics*, © Guardian News and Media Limited 2010.

Chapter Two: Higher Education

Young people's views on Higher Education, © Ipsos MORI, *Did you know? Facts about higher education*, © Universities UK, *Higher education: what will life be like?*, © Uni4me, *2010 university lifestyle survey*, © Sodexo, *50% rise in likelihood of England's poorest teenagers going to university since mid-90s*, © Guardian News and Media Limited 2010, *Fears for 'privatisation' of higher education*, © Voice, *Millennium mothers want university education for their children*, © Centre for Longitudinal Studies, *UCAS reports record student applications for university*, © Guardian News and Media Limited 2010, *Ministers push for more apprenticeships*, © CIPD, *Economic fears get more adults learning*, © NIACE.

Illustrations

Pages 2, 17, 23, 32: Simon Kneebone; pages 6, 11, 19, 30: Angelo Madrid; pages 8, 13, 29, 35: Don Hatcher; pages 5, 36: Bev Aisbett.

Cover photography

Left: © Alicja Stolarczyk. Centre: © Sanja Gjenero. Right: © Miguel Ugalde.

Additional acknowledgements

Editorial by Carolyn Kirby on behalf of Independence.

And with thanks to the Independence team: Mary Chapman, Sandra Dennis and Jan Sunderland.

Lisa Firth
Cambridge
April, 2011

ASSIGNMENTS

The following tasks aim to help you think through the issues surrounding the education debate and provide a better understanding of the topic.

1 In pairs, brainstorm to find out what you know about the education system in Britain. How does it vary between England, Wales, Scotland and Ireland? What compulsory exams must pupils take and when?

2 Read *Attitudes to learning* on page 1. Carry out a survey to find out what pupils in your class think about the different types of learning. Do they prefer vocational or academic learning? Which do you think your school should focus on more?

3 It has been suggested that there is increasing pressure on school pupils to achieve academic success, and that there is now a greater focus on simply training students to pass exams. Write an article for a student newspaper giving your opinion on this topic. Do you think exams are the most important part of school? Or should other factors, such as life skills or students' wellbeing, be taken into consideration?

4 In groups of four, design a large wall poster giving information on the opportunities available to 16-year-old school-leavers. Try to include academic and vocational options. How many can you come up with?

5 Read *Are our schools really failing?* on page 7, and *Myth: standards rise is just exams getting easier* on page 9. You may also choose to carry out your own research into exams now and in the past. As a class, debate the following motion: 'This house believes that exams are now easier than they were 50 years ago.' Half should argue in favour and the other half against

6 Study the graph 'Educational attainment at age 16 by ethnic group' on page 14. What do the results show? Write a summary of your observations and conclusions.

7 Using the Internet, carry out research into the different types of schools available in Britain. How do you think a student's experience of school would differ in a comprehensive state school compared to a fee-paying

independent school? Do you think the Government's recent introduction of 'free schools' is a good idea? Discuss your thoughts with a partner.

8 'It is a teacher's responsibility to teach a child good behaviour and discipline. The child's parents should not be allowed to interfere with this.' Debate this statement in groups of four. Do you agree or disagree with it?

9 Statistics show that social class seems to have a greater influence on White British pupils' educational attainment than any other ethnic group. Why do you think this might be?

10 Visit the BBC's Bitesize revision website at www.bbc.co.uk/schools/gcsebitesize. Do you find it helpful? Write a review of the website, including your views on the site's ease of navigation, the usefulness of the information provided etc.

11 There is a lot of controversy over the source of funding for higher education. Do you think the Government should pay for university education? Or should it be up to the students and their families? And if students are funding their own education, should universities be allowed to charge however much they want? Write down your opinions, then compare your views with the rest of the class.

12 Write a short piece of prose entitled 'A day in the life of a fresher student...' Imagine how a first-year university student may feel during the first few weeks of university, and the things they may do. Would they be excited or nervous? What challenges might they face?

13 Schools and colleges often focus on academic paths for students – providing information and encouragement for them to enter higher education. Carry out research into other opportunities in your area. Can you find any apprenticeships on offer? Or many employment vacancies suitable for a school leaver? Write a list of your findings and compare them with others in your class.

14 Watch the film 'Dead Poets' Society', starring Robin Williams as an inspirational teacher, and write a review.